First published by One More Grain Of Sand, 2015
info@onemoregrainofsand.com

www.secretseeker.com

Research by Jane Sarchet, Brendan Barry, Alex Whittleton and Rob Smith
Photography by Jane Sarchet and Brendan Barry unless otherwise stated below
Book design by Ben Hoo and Rob Smith
Book series design by Ben Hoo
Edited by Katie Halpin and Alex Whittleton
Printed by Cambrian Printers, Aberystwyth, Wales

ISBN: 978-1-910992-06-7

Photo credits: Board and knife p.228 © Destinyweddingstudio; Bath p.232 © JeniFoto; Padstow Harbour p.236 © Ian Woolcock; Panorama of Totnes p.238 © Samot; Lyme Regis harbour p.240 © Ralf Gosch; Frome p.245 © David Michael Bellis & Blue Rock Fox Productions.

Every effort has been made to trace copyright ownership and to obtain permission for reproduction of the images in this book. If you believe you are the copyright owner, and we have not requested your permission, please contact us: info@onemoregrainofsand.com

Help us update: A great deal of effort and many calories went into the making of this book, but if you think something could be improved, or you have a secret recommendation of your own, we'd love to hear from you: info@onemoregrainofsand.com

ONE
MORE
GRAIN
OF
SAND

Secret Kitchen
Southwest England

by Jane Sarchet and Rob Smith
with additional contributions by Alex Whittleton

CONTENTS

	page
Introduction	6
How to use this book	7
Restaurants, Pubs & Cafés	8–147
• Cornwall	10–41
• Devon	42–73
• Dorset	74–95
• Bristol & Bath	96–123
• Somerset	124–147
Delis, Bakeries & Suppliers	148–177
Farms, Markets & Street Food	178–217
Cookery Schools	218–231
Foodie Towns	232–245
Index	246–249
Best Venues For...	250–253
Acknowledgements	254–256

INTRODUCTION

Welcome to *Secret Kitchen: Southwest England*, an insider's guide to the best places to eat, buy and source the finest produce in the West Country. Over recent years, customers have been demanding more sustainably farmed, locally sourced foods, which has led to a rise in artisan growers, producers and sellers. This movement has inspired many farmers to return to time-honoured methods and traditions. And nowhere is this trend more noticeable than in Southwest England, with its deep-rooted farming culture. You'll find plenty of outdoor-reared meat, fresh fish plucked out of the nearby sea and local, organic fruit and veg on the menus of even the smallest cafés.

This book has something for everyone, whatever your budget, tastes or dietary requirements. From elegant fine-dining restaurants, backstreet bistros and earthy street-food sellers to amazing farm shops, delis, bakeries and cookery schools, we are proud to bring you such a vibrant and varied selection of 'Secret Kitchens'. Our choices are based on outstanding produce, service and expertise, or simply because they are endearingly quirky. And while, for obvious reasons, it's impossible to find a truly secret restaurant, we have included places that many locals will not have heard of, and discovered something secret about them.

We have split this book into five main sections and provided a map for each of them so you can see, at a glance, which venues are located near you. The five sections are:

Restaurants, Pubs & Cafés
Delis, Bakeries & Suppliers
Farms, Markets & Street Food
Cookery Schools
Foodie Towns

The Restaurants, Pubs & Cafés section has been split into areas (by county), due to the number of venues covered. Each of these areas has an individual map to make navigation easier.

Each venue is colour coded by county (Cornwall, Devon, Dorset, Bristol & Bath and Somerset). You will find opening times and driving directions and, in the icons and ratings, information about whether the venue caters for food intolerances, is dog friendly or has excellent service. See below.

ICONS

 Gluten-free option

 Vegan option

 Wheelchair access

 Parking

 Dog friendly

 Family venue

 WiFi network

 Outdoor seating

 Sea view

Meal and drink for one person:
£   Under £10
££ Under £20
£££ £20 and over

RATINGS

Venues are rated on service, healthy food and ambience, as shown below on a 1–5 scale.

SERVICE

HEALTHY FOOD

AMBIENCE

Restaurants, Pubs & Cafés

Cornwall
Restaurants, Pubs & Cafés

VENUES

		page
1	The Apple Tree Café	12
2	Heather's Coffee Shop	13
3	The Old Coastguard	14
4	Poolside Indulgence	15
5	Coast Coffee Bar and Bistro	16
6	The Pavilion Boatshed	18
7	Fern Pit Café	20
8	Wildebeest	22
9	The Secret Garden Café	23
10	The Idle Rocks	24
11	Strong Adolfos	28
12	Heligan Tearoom	30
13	The Hidden Hut	32
14	The Kings Arms	33
15	Woods Café	34
16	Masons Arms	35
17	Talland Bay Beach Café	36
18	Ocean & Earth	38
19	The Springer Spaniel	40

The Apple Tree Café
Feed your soul

4
SERVICE

4
HEALTHY
FOOD

4
AMBIENCE

Summer daily 10–5,
winter Thu–Sun 10–4

££

Trevescan, Sennen TR19 7AQ
01736 872 753
www.theappletreecafe.co.uk

Getting There
Head towards Land's End and when
you get to the hamlet of Trevescan,
look out for signs to the café.

The Secret
Tucked away down meandering
Cornish lanes and only half-a-mile
from Land's End, this is the most
westerly secret kitchen in England.

Displaying art in restaurants and cafés is not a new
idea, but The Apple Tree Café does it really well thanks
to the lovely converted barn it occupies and the quality
of the art itself. Pieces by local artists add splashes
of colour to the whitewashed interior, where winter
visitors warm themselves on sofas next to the wood-
burning stove. In the summer, visitors can enjoy the
sunshine at one of the tables in the pretty garden.

Bursting with fresh, vibrant dishes, the menu fulfils the
desires of meat-eaters, but excels when it comes to
satisfying vegetarians. Options include sprouted salads,
homemade coleslaw and even a vegetarian version of
a full 'Cornish' breakfast. The menu covers most food
intolerances, and alterations can happily be made to
dishes by asking the friendly staff.

Speciality: Apple Tree veggie burger with homemade
cider-apple chutney and salad

Heather's Coffee Shop
Coffee & cream tea

Set in an Area of Outstanding Natural Beauty overlooking the sea where meandering footpaths and stone hedgerows have created a patchwork of tiny fields, this friendly tearoom is a favourite with walkers.

Heather and her team use locally sourced ingredients as much as possible, showcasing some of the best Cornish food and drink. Expect splendid breakfasts and light lunches, as well as homemade cakes and Cornish cream teas. Also on offer is what many patrons consider to be the best coffee in Cornwall.

The café occupies the old village store, right in the heart of the village of Pendeen. Its homely, bunting-clad interior has something of the 1940s about it, and the walled courtyard at the back is lovely in summer.

Specialities: cakes, cream teas, coffee

Summer daily 8.30–5.30, winter daily 9–5 £

11 Church Road, Penzance
TR19 7SF, 01736 788 069
facebook.com/
heatherscoffeeshopcornwall

Getting There
Pendeen is on the coastal road from Penzance to St Ives (B3306). You'll find Heather's on your right, at the junction with Church Road.

The Secret
Heather's appears on the Truly Cornish Café Trail – a list of the finest independent cafés in the county.

5 SERVICE

3 HEALTHY FOOD

4 AMBIENCE

The Old Coastguard
Through the picture window

5 SERVICE

5 HEALTHY FOOD

5 AMBIENCE

Daily 12.30–2.30,
3–5.30 & 6.30–9

££

The Parade, Mousehole, Penzance
TR19 6PR, 01736 731 222
www.oldcoastguardhotel.co.uk

Getting There
Once in Mousehole, head along
Parade Hill, where you'll find The
Old Coastguard overlooking the sea.

The Secret
*The team here lives by the maxim
'the best things in life are simple',
and it's hard to disagree when you
sit back with a belly full of great food
and watch the waves roll in.*

The Old Coastguard is just 3km east of Newlyn, and
– as you might expect – there is plenty of seafood on
the menu. In fact, the kitchen exploits all that Cornwall
has to offer, from the freshest local fish and shellfish to
Cornish beef, poultry, game, cheeses and ice creams.

Breakfast is a highlight here. Try the full 'Cornish', the
Newlyn smoked salmon and scrambled eggs, or the
yoghurt with homemade muesli. Or stop by later in the
day for the quirky 'Not Lunch, Not Supper' (3–5pm).

There's a rough-around-the-edges atmosphere at The Old
Coastguard, with its sunny painted walls, comfy sofas and
big oak tables. The huge picture windows and sun terrace
offer spectacular coastal views – and if you look out across
the waves, you may even spot Salty the Seal sunbathing on
nearby St Clement's Island.

Specialities: breakfasts, 'Not Lunch, Not Supper'

G V ♿ 🐾 👨‍👧 📶 🅰 🌊

Poolside Indulgence
Lounging at the lido

When you hear the word lido, you think kids, ice cream and saucy postcards – not, perhaps, a Mediterranean restaurant. But for the people of Penzance, crusty ciabattas, antipasti platters and bowls of pasta spring to mind at the merest mention of an open-air swim, thanks to the proximity of this restaurant to the historic Jubilee Pool. Built in 1935 to celebrate King George V's silver jubilee, this lido is one of the best preserved in the country.

When you arrive at the restaurant, you're met with a sign pointing to the harbour that reads: 'All our seafood comes from over there'. This statement sets the tone for the rest of the menu, which is almost entirely locally sourced. Grab a table on the terrace and enjoy the bay views. And if you visit on a Friday night in summer, you can learn the delicate art of eating a crab with style.

Speciality: Friday Crab Nights

Easter–Oct daily from 10   £

Jubilee Pool, Wharf Road, Penzance
TR18 4HH, 07779 998 590
www.poolside-indulgence.co.uk

Getting There
Heading west on the A30, take the first exit onto the B3311. Continue onto Wharf Road and Poolside Indulgence is on the right.

The Secret
The terrace at Poolside Indulgence offers one of the most spectacular views of St Michael's Mount in town.

4
SERVICE

5
HEALTHY FOOD

4
AMBIENCE

Coast Coffee Bar and Bistro
Coffee on the coast

4 SERVICE

3 HEALTHY FOOD

3 AMBIENCE

Daily 9.30–9

£ to ££

Lighthouse Road, The Lizard,
Helston TR12 7NJ
01326 290 400
www.coastthelizard.co.uk

Getting There
Take the A3083 into The Lizard, and
Coast Coffee Bar is on your right,
after the turn-off for The Square.

The Secret
*Our most southerly secret kitchen
offers day-long lobster-fishing trips
that culminate in an evening feast
featuring the day's catch.*

After a bracing walk on The Lizard, the most southerly
point on the British mainland, a feed at Coast is almost
certainly in order. The seafood served here is about as
fresh as it comes, plucked straight from the swirling
Atlantic waters that surround this rugged peninsula.

The menu also includes meat from the local butcher
and vegetables, salad and eggs from nearby farms.
Traditional cream teas, homemade cakes and coffee
are served throughout the day.

Coast occupies a former Royal National Lifeboat
Institution (RNLI) garage that opens out onto a big,
sunny terrace, which is ideal in warm weather. For
colder, wetter days, you can warm up on a sofa by the
wood-burner with a cup of steaming hot chocolate.

Specialities: fresh fish, burgers, cream teas

The Pavilion Boatshed
You scream ice cream

5 SERVICE

4 HEALTHY FOOD

4 AMBIENCE

Wed–Sat midday–2.30
& 6–9, Sun midday–4

££ to £££

8 Beach Road, Perranporth
TR6 0JL, 01872 300 784
www.thepavilionboatshed.com

Getting There
Take the B3285 into Perranporth and
The Pavilion Boatshed can be found
opposite the large beach car park.

The Secret
*This restaurant has its own brand
of ice cream, Pavilion Ice, which
comes in 30-plus flavours, including
seasonal specials. There are also
sorbets and dog-friendly ice creams.*

The Pavilion Boatshed is a popular restaurant just a
few seconds' walk from the beach. The owner and head
chef, Matt Burrell, cooked his way around the world –
working in Michelin-starred establishments in Australia
and making gelato in Italy – before opening up this
restaurant in his hometown of Perranporth.

The mouthwatering menu is inspired by the rich fishing
waters off the Cornish coast, as well as the county's
farmers and local suppliers. The house speciality is a
fresh seafood platter, Taste of the Sea, which is packed
with masses of fish and shellfish that's simply cooked
and beautifully presented.

Have a glass of champagne or a local ale by the big
beachfront windows or on the street outside if it's sunny,
and watch the surf crowd go by.

Specialities: Taste of the Sea, dog-friendly ice creams

Fern Pit Café
Seafood, sarnies & sun

5 SERVICE

3 HEALTHY FOOD

5 AMBIENCE

Summer daily 10–5, winter opening may vary **£**

19 Riverside Crescent, Pentire, Newquay TR7 1PJ, 01637 873 181
www.fernpit.co.uk

Getting There
From the A392, turn left at the roundabout onto Pentire Road, then onto Pentire Avenue, then Riverside Crescent; follow signs to the ferry.

The Secret
The ferry boathouse appears in three photos in The Who's 1973 album, Quadrophenia. The rowing boat in one of them, Hope, can still be seen today.

Fern Pit Café boasts extraordinary views out over the River Gannel to the open sea beyond. It lies on the Newquay side of the Pentire headland, overlooking Crantock beach, which can be accessed via a little wooden bridge from Crantock Bay at low tide.

This friendly, family-run café, which dates back to 1910, is a great place for breakfast, lunch or a snack. On the menu are traditional Cornish cream teas, homemade cakes and sandwiches generously filled with prawns and freshly caught crab.

During the summer, a ferry runs between the boathouse just below the café, Crantock beach and Newquay. At the boathouse, you can buy locally caught live lobsters and crabs or order them cooked. Feel free to ask for advice on preparing the catch at home.

Specialities: crab sandwiches, cream teas

Wildebeest
Green feast

5
SERVICE

4
HEALTHY
FOOD

3
AMBIENCE

Mon & Wed–Sat midday–3 & 6–9, Sun 11–4 **£**

13 Arwenack Street, Falmouth
TR11 3JD, 01326 210 602
www.wildebeestcafe.com

Getting There
Wildebeest is on Arwenack Street, the main shopping street in Falmouth. There's parking at either end of town, and it's a pleasant walk to the café.

The Secret
From recycling and composting to biodegradable food packaging and even carbon-neutral web-hosting, this café is enviably green and clean.

If you struggle to find inspiring vegan food when eating out, then this place is likely to knock your socks off. Its mainly Japanese- and Mexican-inspired dishes use the freshest seasonal produce in such tasty combinations that even the most ardent meat-lovers are likely to feel satisfied.

Mouthwatering raw-food creations loom large on the menu, and include the likes of cucumber and shaved-asparagus salad with hoisin sauce, peanuts and a hot ginger dressing. There's also a great choice of cakes and desserts – try the warm chocolate brownie.

Tea and coffee at Wildebeest are served with a choice of dairy-free milk alternatives, including soya milk, and all wines and spirits are organic.

Specialities: vegan cheesecake, raw Pad Thai, pear and cardamom ice cream

The Secret Garden Café
Healthy hideaway

The elegant Georgian frontage of The Secret Garden Café gives way to an inviting interior that's modern, relaxed and buzzing with atmosphere. Owned by Sasha – who trained at the award-winning Ashburton Cookery School – and her partner, Ben, the café is the result of months of dreaming and planning while creating great-tasting food on a campervan stove in New Zealand.

The menu is mostly vegetarian and features tasty lunchtime dishes such as smoky-roasted beetroot and black-bean burger with salad, harissa mayo and hand-cut potato wedges. Fun labels on the menu let diners know how many of their five-a-day are in any given dish.

And, as an antidote to all that virtuous veg, don't forget to visit the Naughty Corner for some delicious, decadent treats.

Speciality: smoky-roasted beetroot and black-bean burger

Mon–Sat 10.30–4.30   £

15 Kenwyn Street, Truro TR1 3BU
07949 293 399
www.secretgardencafe.co.uk

Getting There
The Secret Garden Café is tucked away on Kenwyn Street, a gentle walk from the hustle and bustle of Truro city centre.

The Secret
The name's the giveaway! This café has a secluded garden tucked around the back decorated with mirrors, shrubs and flower-bedecked cherubs.

SERVICE

HEALTHY
FOOD

AMBIENCE

The Idle Rocks
A place in the sun

4
SERVICE

5
HEALTHY FOOD

4
AMBIENCE

Daily from 8

££ to £££

Harbourside, St Mawes
TR2 5AN, 01326 270 270
www.idlerocks.com

Getting There
The Idle Rocks is on the A3078,
overlooking the harbour in St Mawes.

The Secret
*Desserts can be ordered in
half-portions here – perfect for
youngsters and anyone trying to
minimise their holiday-eating guilt.*

Set right on St Mawes harbour opposite the Idle Rocks themselves, this stylish boutique hotel is known for its outstanding restaurant. Offering fresh, local and seasonal ingredients, simply cooked and served in a jaw-dropping setting, this is seaside dining at its best.

In summer, tables empty out onto a south-facing terrace where elegant parasols provide shade from the sun. The atmosphere here, with the background sounds of music, chatter and boating activity in the harbour, is lively but very relaxed – especially when you have a chilled glass of wine or a cocktail in hand.

Non-residents are always welcome in the restaurant, which – although it may not be cheap – makes for an unforgettable treat.

Speciality: ceviche, globe-artichoke tart

Sunny terrace at The Idle Rocks

Strong Adolfos
Bikes & burgers

SERVICE 5

HEALTHY FOOD 4

AMBIENCE 4

Mon–Fri 8.30–4.30,
Sat & Sun 9–5

£ to ££

Hawksfield A39, Wadebridge
PL27 7LR, 01208 816 949
www.strongadolfos.com

Getting There
Heading south out of town on the A39, Strong Adolfos is on your right, just past the turn-off for the A389.

The Secret
According to its droves of fans, Strong Adolfos serves the best bacon and maple-syrup pancakes in England – a far cry from the limp bacon butties served up at many a roadside café.

Fresh, friendly and retro cool, Strong Adolfos serves classic burgers and sliders along with tasty dahl, soups, salads and ever-changing specials. The wine list is limited but well researched, and there are local ales and craft beers to sample.

If you fancy an alternative to the traditional cream tea, then Strong Adolfos brings you cracking coffee and cakes. In fact, it takes its coffee-making very seriously indeed – almost to the point of nerdiness. The science is in the brewing, the art is in the delivery.

The running theme at this restaurant is 'art, surf and motorcycles'. An exhibition space displays the work of emerging artists, photographers and illustrators, and there are regular motorcycle nights. Other offerings include a classic-car club and live-music events.

Specialities: burgers, coffee, homemade cakes

Heligan Tearoom
Tea in the garden

3 SERVICE

4 HEALTHY FOOD

4 AMBIENCE

Daily 9.30–4.30   £

Pentewan, St Austell PL26 6EN
01726 845 100
www.heligan.com

Getting There
From St Austell, take the B3273
towards Mevagissey. At the top of
the huge hill you climb, turn right
and follow the signs to Heligan.

The Secret
*Most of the fresh produce served
in the tearoom here is grown on site.
Forget food miles – we're talking 150
or so food yards from soil to plate.*

People come from far and wide to eat in the award-
winning tearoom at the Lost Gardens of Heligan. The
menu revolves around a superb array of heirloom fruit
and veg, from summer salads to warming winter stews.

The Sunday roasts here are renowned, and well worth
splashing out on if you don't fancy cooking your own.
The cakes and scones are also delicious, so if you
miss the lunch slot (midday–2.30), you can fill up on
an indulgent cream tea.

In winter, the wood-burning stove becomes a focal
point inside, while in the summer, visitors make a
beeline for the abundant outdoor seating.

There's a charge to visit the gardens, but we highly
recommend that you do – they are truly magical.

Specialities: Sunday roasts, cream teas

The Hidden Hut
Beachside bonanza

5
SERVICE

4
HEALTHY FOOD

5
AMBIENCE

Summer daily 10–5, winter weekends only

£

Porthcurnick Beach, Portscatho, Truro TR2 5EW
www.hiddenhut.co.uk

Getting There
Park at Porthcurnick Beach car park in Portscatho and take a short walk (across 2 fields) towards the beach. Ignore the steps down to the beach and carry on up over the brow of the hill.

The Secret
A small café by day and a pop-up feast venue by night, this is a beach hut with a difference.

They like to keep things simple at The Hut, so expect down-to-earth, seasonal fare. Homemade Cornish pasties, sausage rolls and cakes tend to be typical daytime offerings, but if the weather's nice, you may come across an impromptu barbecue or paella party.

The café also puts on regular feast nights throughout the warmer months, when exotic recipes such as Moroccan spiced lamb are cooked on a charcoal grill outside. Remember to wrap up warm for these – it can get nippy on the beach at sundown.

As its name suggests, The Hidden Hut is somewhat tucked away, just off the coast path on the Roseland Peninsula. The fact that you can't drive here adds to the sense of seclusion and charm, although it makes it hard to access for those with walking difficulties.

Specialities: Cornish pasties, feast nights

The Kings Arms
Like pubs used to be

If you're bored of swanky gastro pubs and in need of some honest, home-cooked food, you can't go wrong with The Kings Arms, which serves a great choice of classic pub grub and a fine selection of local ales.

All the trappings of a typical locals' pub can be found here, from the pool table, dartboard and skittle alley to the heavily patterned carpets. But it's an excellent pitstop for hungry walkers, cyclists and families, with a daily-changing specials board and popular 'build your own burger' option.

Above all, The Kings Arms is a fun place to be. On the first Wednesday of the month, it hosts a Cornish music and dance night, and during Mevagissey's midsummer Feast Week Festival, live bands and the infamous Ball Race take place here.

Speciality: butternut-squash Wellington

Mon–Thu 11–11,
Fri–Sun 11–midnight

££

Bridges, Luxulyan PL30 5EF
01726 850 202
www.staustellbrewery.co.uk/pub/
luxulyan/kings-arms

Getting There
From the A30, take the A391 towards St Austell. Follow the signs towards Luxulyan, and The Kings Arms can be found just over the railway bridge.

The Secret
It's possible to walk to this pub from the UNESCO-listed Luxulyan Valley and the world-famous Eden Project.

5
SERVICE

3
HEALTHY FOOD

3
AMBIENCE

Woods Café
A woodland welcome

3 SERVICE

3 HEALTHY FOOD

5 AMBIENCE

Daily 10.30–4.30, with extended summer hours   **£**

Cardinham Woods, Bodmin
PL30 4AL, 01208 781 11
www.woodscafecornwall.co.uk

Getting There
Cardinham Woods are to the east of Bodmin. Once in the woods, head to the main car park and the café is close by and well signposted.

The Secret
You wouldn't know it, but there's a newly refurbished, two-bedroom apartment to rent above this little café. See website for details.

The pretty, stonework Woods Café in the centre of Cardinham Woods is ready to tend to the needs of weary walkers with cakes, freshly baked scones and a tempting lunch menu. Some regulars make the trip here for the delicious pulled-pork ciabatta alone.

In the café's large woodland garden, which is lovely in summer, there are plenty of tables and water bowls for thirsty dogs. In winter, weather-beaten walkers make straight for the seats nearest the roaring log fire, savouring hot chocolates and warming bowls of soup.

The surrounding woods are perfect for those with boisterous dogs or kids to wear out – or for anyone who has eaten one too many pasties on holiday and needs to stretch their legs. You'll find a playground and several walking and cycling trails here.

Specialities: cheese scones, pulled-pork baguette

Masons Arms
Rabbit! Rabbit! Rabbit!

When visiting the Masons Arms, we recommend ignoring the regular menu in favour of the impressive specials board. Typical dishes include lamb's liver with bacon and onion gravy and a Rabbit Duo – rabbit pie and pan-fried rabbit loin in a wine sauce with Dauphinoise potatoes and seasonal veg. A separate fish menu celebrates locally landed seafood, and there are plenty of options for vegetarians.

Run by the same team for 20 years, the pub is known for its ever-expanding collection of interesting artefacts and quirky memorabilia that – quite literally – covers the interior (including the ceiling). The result is rather chaotic, but also very charming.

In good weather, the beer garden, which backs onto the River Camel, fills up fast. Dogs on leads are welcome.

Specialities: home-reared lamb, seafood, game

Daily midday–2.30 & 6–9   ££

Market Place, Camelford PL32 9PB
01840 213 309
www.masonsarmscamelford.co.uk

Getting There
The Masons Arms is easily located on Market Place (A39) in Camelford. Conveniently, there is a public car park just a short walk away.

The Secret
If you're celebrating a special occasion, call ahead and the landlady, Jo, and her team will decorate the table and organise a cake for you.

SERVICE

HEALTHY FOOD

AMBIENCE

Talland Bay Beach Café
Beside the seaside

(3) SERVICE

(3) HEALTHY FOOD

(4) AMBIENCE

Mid-Mar–end Oct
daily 9–5.30

£

Talland, Looe PL13 2JA
01503 272 088
www.tallandbaybeachcafe.co.uk

Getting There
On the Looe-to-Polperro road (A387),
simply follow the signs to Talland Bay.
The lanes are very narrow in places,
so drive with extra caution.

The Secret
*This café has an on-site beach shop
that offers a kayak-hire service; the
kayaks are single-seaters, but can
hold an adult with a small child.*

This café has huge appeal, thanks to its beautiful
beachside location, outstanding views, lovely food and
quirky seating areas. Opt for a stool by the big windows
overlooking the beach, a bench beneath a bright-blue
parasol or one of the beautifully decorated beach huts
that are kitted out with shabby-chic tables and chairs.

When it comes to food at Talland Bay Beach Café,
expect light bites: paninis, pasties and soup, cakes,
cream teas and Cornish ice creams. The coffee is
freshly ground and really good.

The small pebbly beach in front of the café is very
sheltered and great for kids. It's the perfect place for
swimming, exploring rock pools and kayaking. At low
tide, a giant sandbank appears, which provides no end
of paddling and sandcastle fun.

Specialities: ice creams, coffee, homemade cakes

Ocean & Earth
Heaven on a plate

5 SERVICE

5 HEALTHY FOOD

4 AMBIENCE

Summer Mon–Sat 5–11,
Sun 6–10.30

££

Higher Market Street, East Looe
PL13 1BF, 01503 263 080
www.oceanandearththairestaurant.co.uk

Getting There
Wander through the streets of Looe
down towards the beach, taking the
left turn at Mountain Warehouse onto
Higher Market Street.

The Secret
*This exceptional restaurant offers
a catering service for functions
and dinner parties, in your own
home or elsewhere.*

Anyone who has visited Thailand and misses its fragrant
cuisine should eat at Ocean & Earth. This intimate and
beautifully decorated restaurant blends the very best
local ingredients with signature Asian flavours, creating
mouthwatering Thai fare with a lovely Cornish twist.

You'll find old favourites on the menu, such as Pad Thai
noodles with a zingy papaya salad and Thai green curry
with coconut milk and fresh spices. The chefs are very
imaginative with their specials, bringing diners some
refreshingly unusual combinations.

Occasionally, the restaurant hosts special events to
celebrate festivals in the Thai calendar. These evenings
tend to be very popular, so it's advisable to book ahead.
If you're too late, however, there's always the excellent
takeaway service.

Specialities: Thai green curry, Tom Yam Gai

The Springer Spaniel
All in the game

4

SERVICE

3

HEALTHY FOOD

4

AMBIENCE

Mon–Sat midday–3 & 6–9   ££

Treburley, Launceston PL15 9NS
01579 370 424
www.thespringerspaniel.co.uk

Getting There
The Springer Spaniel is situated on the A388 between Callington and Launceston.

The Secret
The owner of The Springer Spaniel is none other than the Masterchef 2012 winner, Anton Piotrowski, who has big plans for this 18th-century pub.

The Springer Spaniel is a traditional country pub with a welcoming, lively atmosphere and crackling open fires. And with several menus to choose from, it's a top choice for families and big groups.

For a slap-up lunch, try the upmarket yet classic bar menu, with its steak sandwich with fried egg and triple-cooked chips – artery-clogging but utterly delicious. There's also a menu for kids (otherwise known as 'Springer pups') and a spectacular fine-dining taster menu, which features seven courses.

There's an emphasis on game at this pub, as its hunting-inspired décor suggests, with duck, venison, guinea fowl and pheasant dishes making regular appearances on the menu. And though the food is classy, the atmosphere remains unpretentious.

Specialities: game, desserts

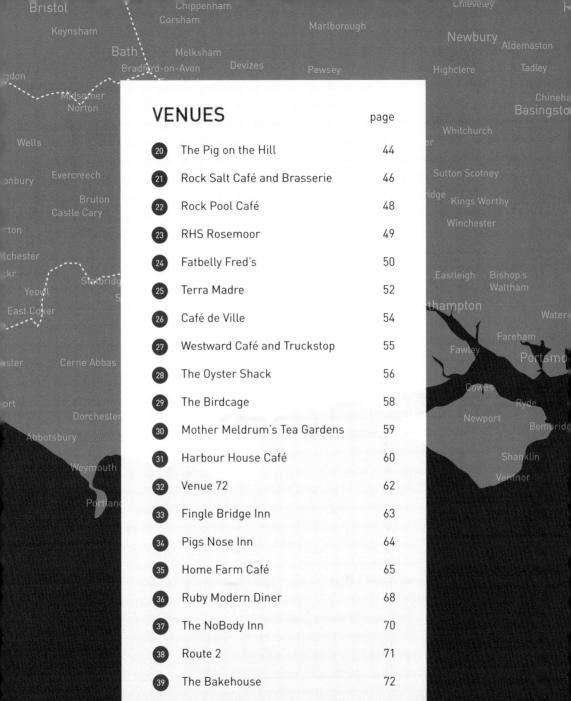

VENUES

		page
20	The Pig on the Hill	44
21	Rock Salt Café and Brasserie	46
22	Rock Pool Café	48
23	RHS Rosemoor	49
24	Fatbelly Fred's	50
25	Terra Madre	52
26	Café de Ville	54
27	Westward Café and Truckstop	55
28	The Oyster Shack	56
29	The Birdcage	58
30	Mother Meldrum's Tea Gardens	59
31	Harbour House Café	60
32	Venue 72	62
33	Fingle Bridge Inn	63
34	Pigs Nose Inn	64
35	Home Farm Café	65
36	Ruby Modern Diner	68
37	The NoBody Inn	70
38	Route 2	71
39	The Bakehouse	72

The Pig on the Hill
Piggy pub grub

5
SERVICE

4
HEALTHY FOOD

5
AMBIENCE

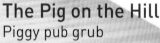

Daily from 11   ££

Pusehill Road, Westward Ho!
EX39 5AH, 01237 459 222
www.pigonthehillwestwardho.co.uk

Getting There
Heading towards Barnstable on the
A39, take the B3236 towards Westward
Ho!. Turn left onto Cornborough Road,
and left again onto Pusehill Road.

The Secret
*The Pig on the Hill is named
after a Vietnamese pot-bellied
pig called Saigon who used to
roam this very spot.*

The Pig on The Hill occupies a converted cowshed
set in beautiful countryside only a short distance
from the sea. With its down-to-earth atmosphere
and good-quality food, the pub has a loyal band of
regulars from across the local area.

The chefs stop at nothing in search of outstanding
ingredients. One of the most sought-after lunch
options is The Pig Club: a sandwich generously filled
with slow-cooked leg of pork, chorizo, grain mustard,
tomato and English leaf salad, and served with fries.
Several interesting vegetarian dishes are also on offer.

The Pig on the Hill is at the heart of the community,
with its games room, skittle alley and Pigstock festival
– a celebration of local music usually held in May.

Specialities: The Pig Club, suckling pig, vegetarian mains

Rock Salt Café and Brasserie
Seven-course heaven

SERVICE 5

HEALTHY FOOD 5

AMBIENCE 5

Sun–Fri 10–9.30,
Sat 8–9.30

££

31 Stonehouse Street, Plymouth
PL1 3PE, 01752 225 522
www.rocksaltcafe.co.uk

Getting There
Take the A374 out of Plymouth, turn
left up the one-way side street next to
the Lidl supermarket, and Rock Salt is
at the top on the right-hand side.

The Secret
*Rock Salt keeps bagging all kinds of
awards, from a Taste of the West gold
award to two coveted AA rosettes.
What will be next for this rising star?*

It's unlikely you'd stumble upon Rock Salt by chance,
given its position off the main drag. But soon after it
opened in 2011, this neighbourhood brasserie was
absolutely buzzing thanks to the power of word of mouth.

The lunch menu features an outstanding beef burger
served with mature cheddar, while the more elaborate
evening menu features venison with braised ox cheek,
bone marrow and red cabbage. Those who fancy
skipping meat altogether have lots of options, from the
black bream with Jerusalem artichoke to the 'forest
fungi' cannelloni with blue cheese.

Finally, for gourmets – hungry ones, at that! – there's
a seven-course tasting menu available every night.
Be sure to book this – and Rock Salt's regular
Pan-Asian evenings – well in advance.

Specialities: burgers, seven-course tasting menu

Rock Pool Café
A fab fry-up

SERVICE 4

HEALTHY FOOD 3

AMBIENCE 3

Daily 9–5 £

2 Golf Links Road, Westward Ho!
EX39 1LH, 01237 477 763
www.facebook.com/
RockPoolCafeWestwardHo

Getting There
This café is next to the Co-Operative
supermarket, opposite the car park,
at Golf Links Road's western end.

The Secret
*This humble little café lies just a few
steps from a golden sandy beach that
stretches for a jaw-dropping 3km.*

This busy seafront café is famous locally for its fry-ups
– real crowd-pleasers that come with eggs, bacon,
sausages, mushrooms, baked beans, buttered toast,
golden hash browns and even chips. Feel free to chop
and change ingredients, depending on what you fancy.

Also a great place for lunch, the café offers baguettes,
paninis, homemade soup and delicious muffins and
cakes. Or, for something more substantial, opt for one
of the classic hot meals, such as the ham, egg and
chips or bangers and mash.

Rock Pool Café is a top choice with families and surfers
on their way to and from the beach that dominates
Westward Ho!. Incidentally, this is the only place in the
UK with a name that includes an exclamation mark.

Specialities: cooked breakfasts, paninis,
homemade soups

RHS Rosemoor
A perfect picnic

Being a Royal Horticultural Society (RHS) garden, Rosemoor may not exactly be a secret, but we had to include it in this guide because of the award-winning food served in its on-site restaurant.

Every day, there are three hot main courses to choose from; these always include a vegetarian and a gluten-free option. Sandwiches, jacket potatoes and masses of fresh produce from the gardens also feature heavily.

While carveries don't always have a great reputation, the one here on Sundays (midday–3) is very good, and usually includes Exmoor-reared beef as one of the two meat choices. The half-portions of hot meals (which are half the price, naturally) are ideal for smaller people.

Entrance to the restaurant is free all year, but please note there is a charge to access the gardens.

Specialities: Sunday roasts, homemade cakes

Apr–Sep daily 10–5.30,
Oct–Mar daily 10–4.30

££

4

SERVICE

RHS Garden Rosemoor, Great Torrington
EX38 8PH, 0845 265 8072
www.rhs.org.uk/gardens/rosemoor

Getting There
Head south out of Great Torrington on the A3124 towards Winkleigh, and the entrance to RHS Rosemoor will be on your right.

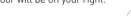

4

HEALTHY
FOOD

The Secret
Order a picnic from the restaurant and go off into the gardens to enjoy the lovely selection of homemade treats outside. The jute picnic bags are reusable – an added bonus!

4

AMBIENCE

Fatbelly Fred's
Seafood sauciness

4

SERVICE

4

HEALTHY FOOD

3

AMBIENCE

Tue–Sat 10–3 & 6–10   £££

16 Maiden Street, Barnstaple
EX31 1HA, 01271 345 700
www.fatbellyfreds.co.uk

Getting There
Fatbelly Fred's is on Maiden Street,
a pedestrianised lane right in the
centre of Barnstable.

The Secret
*This tiny restaurant was named after
the owner's baby son, who had a little
round belly after eating. Apparently, the
big belly now only applies to the owner,
'and not necessarily after eating'.*

If you love seafood, you'll love Fatbelly Fred's. The
menu is one big celebration of the daily catch, with
dishes prepared by seasoned chefs who understand
the intricacies involved in cooking seafood to perfection.

All dishes can be tailored to your taste, so if you don't
fancy a particular sauce or side with your fish, you can
simply swap it for something else. The kitchen is more
than happy to oblige, which is ideal for pernickety eaters
or those with food intolerances.

And if seafood's not your thing, don't worry – there's
always a handful of alternatives, such as the delicious
pan-fried duck breast or the rich aubergine and courgette
bake. It's a good idea to put a call through before you
arrive, so you know what to expect that day.

Specialities: seafood platter, squid with aioli,
mussels Provençal

Terra Madre
The art of tapas

5
SERVICE

5
HEALTHY FOOD

5
AMBIENCE

Wed–Sun 12.30–1.30, also Wed–Sat 7–8.30   ££

Broomhill Art Hotel, Muddiford Road, Barnstaple EX31 4EX, 01271 850 262
www.broomhillart.co.uk

Getting There
Take the A39 north out of Barnstable, then turn left onto the B3230 towards Ilfracombe, following the signs after the North Devon District Hospital.

The Secret
Broomhill offers a range of gift ideas, including a three-course supper and overnight stay. See website for details.

Broomhill, which is situated in the heart of the north Devon countryside, combines a hotel and restaurant with a sculpture garden. This beautifully designed open-air 'gallery', which dates from 1997, features a permanent collection of contemporary sculpture, including the striking *Big Red Shoe* by Greta Berlin, which sits at the hotel entrance.

Just as much of a joy as the art is the food served in Terra Madre, the award-winning on-site restaurant. Mediterranean slow food is the running theme here, with dishes made using organic ingredients from local farms. The three-dish tapas and homemade bread is delicious, while high tea (Wed–Fri 2.30–3.30) is a very civilised affair featuring homemade cakes and snacks. The restaurant is only open on certain days of the week, so booking is essential.

Specialities: tapas, charcuterie, high tea

Café de Ville
The heart of Hatherleigh

4

SERVICE

3

HEALTHY FOOD

4

AMBIENCE

Tue, Thu & Fri 9–5,
Wed & Sat 9–2:30

£

1 Market Street, Hatherleigh
EX20 3JN, 01837 810 582

Getting There
Café de Ville is just a 2-minute walk from a large public car park in the centre of Hatherleigh.

The Secret
When you find a café with a deli attached to it, you know the food will be taken seriously – this place is no exception. Be sure to stock up on larder goodies on your way out.

Café de Ville is a sweet café in the heart of the market town of Hatherleigh. It's usually full of walkers and cyclists in need of quick calories after a session on the nearby Tarka Trail – a 290km track following the route of Tarka the Otter in Henry Williamson's novel of the same name.

The menu offers traditional café meals, from soup, pasties, sandwiches and jacket potatoes to cakes and cream teas. The breakfast menu includes porridge and syrup, an all-day full English, and pretty well everything in between.

If you get there early enough and the weather is fine, grab a table in the lovely little courtyard around the back. Dogs are welcome.

Specialities: pasties, homemade cakes, coffee.

Westward Café and Truckstop
A proper caff

While you won't get a fine-dining experience at Westward Café and Truckstop, you're guaranteed some hearty English café food and the warmest of welcomes.

Dishes on offer here are of the stick-to-your-ribs variety, including homemade cottage pie, liver and bacon casserole and roast dinners. Portion sizes are generous and the café is clean, bright and reminiscent of one of the better greasy spoons of days gone by.

This is a great place to break a long journey to the West Country – it opens its doors very early in the morning and is much cheaper than your average service station. And no need to worry about parking because this is, first and foremost, a lorry drivers' café, so there's ample parking for cars and caravans.

Specialities: chip butties, full English breakfast

Mon–Thu 6–7.30,
Fri 6–2.30, Sat 8–2.30

£

Lee Mill Bridge, Ivybridge PL21 9EE
01752 894 344

Getting There
Turn off the A38 at Lee Mill and the Westward Café and Truckstop is attached to the Gulf petrol station on Plymouth Road.

The Secret
There's nothing particularly glamorous about this roadside café, but if you're after a decent fry-up on the road, you can't beat it.

5
SERVICE

3
HEALTHY
FOOD

2
AMBIENCE

The Oyster Shack
Sensational shellfish

5

SERVICE

5

HEALTHY FOOD

5

AMBIENCE

Daily midday–9 £££

Milburn Orchard Farm, Bigbury
TQ7 4BE, 01548 810 876
www.oystershack.co.uk

Getting There
The restaurant is on Stakes Hill, just
off the A379 on the way to Kingsbridge.
This is a tidal road; at high tide, come
via the hamlet of St Anns Chapel.

The Secret
*If you want to learn how to shuck
oysters and prepare fish, sign up for
one of the day-long Shack Fishing
Trips. See website for details.*

Twenty-five years ago, The Oyster Shack was just that
– a very basic shack where locally caught oysters were
cleaned in tanks before going to market. Locals would
pitch up outside with picnic blankets, crusty bread and
a bottle or two of wine to enjoy a long alfresco lunch
featuring some of the freshest oysters in the southwest.

In a way, not a lot has changed since then. Though
it was turned into a restaurant a few years ago, the
Shack's distinctive heart and soul remain very much
intact. This is a place where friends gather on tables
under awning made from a bright orange sail to share
simple but sensational shellfish.

While you're here, visit the fishmonger's counter,
where you can buy the freshest fish and shellfish
at market prices.

Specialities: crab soup, moules marinière, gravadlax

The Birdcage
Pizza paradise

5

SERVICE

4

HEALTHY FOOD

5

AMBIENCE

Mon–Thu 8.30–5, Fri & Sat 8.30–10, Sun 10–5   £

11 The Square, Chagford TQ13 8AA
01647 433 883
www.thebirdcagechagford.co.uk

Getting There
This café is easily found in Chagford's main square. There are a handful of parking spaces right outside, although they tend to fill up fast.

The Secret
The pizzas here are out of this world – just one reason The Birdcage has been awarded a much sought-after TripAdvisor Certificate of Excellence.

The Birdcage, on the main square in the Dartmoor town of Chagford, is something of a pilgrimage site for gourmet-pizza lovers. Available with gluten-free bases and in two sizes (9 and 12 inches), the pizzas come with a dozen or so different toppings to choose from.

The Rosso Bianco is particularly good, with rosemary-infused mascarpone sauce, mozzarella, juicy sun-blush tomatoes and sweet peppers. The kitchen is happy to swap toppings around, so don't be afraid to ask. If pizza's not your thing, the daily brunch, lunch and afternoon-tea menus have lots of variety and the Friday and Saturday tapas nights are superb.

If the weather's fine, sit at one of the outside tables under a sunshade. Otherwise, enjoy the richly coloured fabrics and quirky design details of the interior.

Specialities: pizzas, cakes, gluten-free dishes

Mother Meldrum's Tea Gardens
Tea in the valley

The Valley of the Rocks is one of the most breathtaking beauty spots in the southwest. It's a big hit with walkers, photographers and other outdoor enthusiasts. Rather unusually, this steep basin runs parallel to the coast.

Mother Meldrum's Tea Gardens are tucked away at the bottom of the valley, surrounded by stunning scenery and watched over by the feral goats who roam the hills. It's a convenient spot for passers-by in need of a pick-me-up. Tuck into homemade pasties, sandwiches and all manner of sweet treats, including cream teas with huge scones and mincemeat and apple lattices. Also on offer are early-evening meals and a roast lunch on Sundays.

The large garden has plenty of picnic tables and is ideal for those with dogs. Inside, there's more seating, although take note: it can get very busy in the high season.

Specialities: cream teas, homemade pasties, cakes

Mid-Mar–end Oct daily 10–5   **££**

The Valley of the Rocks, Lee Toad, Lynton EX35 6JH, 01598 753 667

Getting There
Take the road out of Lynton towards the Valley of the Rocks. As you head down the hill, Mother Meldrum's is hidden in a little piece of woodland on the right-hand side.

The Secret
Steeped in legend, this café is named after a folkloric witch who is said to have lived in the valley. Look out for the witch paraphernalia dotted around.

5
SERVICE

4
HEALTHY FOOD

5
AMBIENCE

Harbour House Café
Deep breath... and relax

5 **SERVICE**

5 **HEALTHY FOOD**

4 **AMBIENCE**

Mon–Sat 10–5   £

Harbour House, The Promenade,
Kingsbridge TQ7 1JD
01548 855 666
www.harbourhousecafe.com

Getting There
Head down Fore Street and onto the
Promenade (A379). The café is on the left.

The Secret
*The sun-lit interior balcony is the best
place to sit at Harbour House Café
– it overlooks the local artworks in
the gallery below. In good weather,
the secluded garden is also lovely.*

The light and airy Harbour House Café is just a short distance from the pretty estuary in the market town of Kingsbridge. The town's only entirely vegetarian establishment, the café uses fresh, seasonal, organic and mainly allotment-grown ingredients in its dishes.

Light lunches here include healthy tagines and tarts, paninis and pittas, soups and salads. The long list of cakes that takes up half the menu is testament to the owners' belief in the benefits of the occasional sugary indulgence. And, as you'd expect, there's lots of choice for vegans and those with food intolerances.

The café is part of the Harbour House Arts & Yoga Centre, which also includes three yoga studios and an art gallery, set in a lovely converted Georgian building.

Specialities: paninis, salads, cakes

Venue 72
Bringing home the bacon

4

SERVICE

4

HEALTHY
FOOD

4

AMBIENCE

Mon–Thu 7–7, Fri & Sat
7–11, Sun 9–5   ££

72 South Street, South Molton
EX36 4AG, 01769 573 274
www.venue72.co.uk

Getting There
South Street is easy to access on
the B3226, one of the main streets
running through town. There's street
parking and a car park near by.

The Secret
*If you're too busy for a sit-down meal
at Bistro 72, either grab a takeaway
or – if you work in town – have your
meal delivered straight to your office.*

Apologies to all the other bacon-butty experts in North
Devon, but, according to Venue 72's regular customers,
the one on the menu here tops the list. Also legendary
are the full English breakfasts and the rather more
sophisticated eggs Benedict.

However, it's the seasonal bistro menu – available on
Friday and Saturday evenings – that really wins the
day at Venue 72. A typical dish might be pan-fried duck
breast served with a traditional Irish colcannon and
local, seasonal veg. Some dishes on the menu are
marked as 'slimming'; though they might be light on
calories, they're still as tasty as anything.

Eating at Venue 72, where you can bring your own
alcohol at weekends, is rather like dining with friends
– lively, relaxed and very good fun.

Specialities: bacon butties, full English breakfast

Fingle Bridge Inn
Old-fashioned pub grub

Perched on the banks of the River Teign, the Fingle Bridge Inn is in such a beautiful setting that you might be tempted to stay longer than planned. This traditional, family-run pub is close to several fairly easy walks along the river, which are ideal for families.

On the menu, you'll find good, old-fashioned pub grub, including classics such as ham, egg and chips, steak and ale pie and ploughman's lunches. For something a bit lighter, try a bar snack – delicious washed down with a locally brewed ale or cider – or a Devon cream tea (served midday–5). The renowned Sunday carvery gets very busy, so it's best to book ahead.

In winter, log fires warm the cosy interior, while balmy summer days are best spent on the riverside terrace.

Specialities: Sunday carvery, cream teas, ploughman's lunches

Daily midday–3 & 6–9   £

Drewsteignton EX6 6PW
01647 281 287
www.finglebridgeinn.co.uk

Getting There
From Exeter, take the A30 westbound. At Woodleigh junction, follow the signs to Crockernwell and then onwards to Fingle Bridge.

The Secret
The Fingle Bridge Inn has a large function room that can accommodate 120 people – ideal for weddings, parties, conferences and other events.

4
SERVICE

4
HEALTHY FOOD

5
AMBIENCE

Pigs Nose Inn
In a world of its own

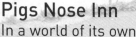

(5)
SERVICE

(3)
HEALTHY
FOOD

(4)
AMBIENCE

Daily midday–2 & 6.30/7–9
(closed Sun eve in winter)   £

East Prawle, Kingsbridge
TQ7 2BY, 01548 511 209
www.pigsnoseinn.co.uk

Getting There
East Prawle is on the southernmost
tip of Devon and the Pigs Nose Inn is
in the centre of the village, opposite
Piglet Stores, the village shop.

The Secret
*The Pigs Nose Inn, which dates
back 500 years, was once a
smugglers' inn where booty from
local shipwrecks was stored.*

Entering the Pigs Nose, you feel like you've stepped into
an alternative reality. Every corner, shelf and surface is
bursting with knick-knacks and odd curiosities, from
abandoned bits of knitting just waiting to be picked up and
continued to sun-bleached animal skulls. Every artefact
has a story – just ask at the bar if you'd like to know more.

The meals served at the Pigs Nose are the definition of
basic, filling slap-up food – think chilli con carne, scampi
and chips, and ploughman's lunches – and the hand-
pumped beers are wonderful. Good news all round, when
you consider the pub's proximity to the coast path and the
many campsites that spring up in nearby fields in summer.

The pub is the beating heart of the village of East Prawle.
It overlooks the pretty village green and the village shop
– the equally eccentric Piglet Stores.

Specialities: paella, chilli con carne, fish and chips

Home Farm Café
Simplicity & style

The elegant country estate of Parke is situated on the edge of Bovey Tracey, with the wild expanse of Dartmoor beyond. Its acres of meadows, gardens and parkland are a great place to work up an appetite before heading to the on-site café for a lovely lazy lunch.

Home Farm Café is run by Stella West-Harling MBE, founder of the acclaimed Ashburton Cookery School, whose passion for genuine, earthy food is renowned.

Menu highlights include jacket potatoes with generous fillings and slow-cooked beef pasties. Evening meals, which are eaten by candlelight, put Dartmoor firmly in the spotlight, with locally raised beef, pork and lamb featuring heavily. Although not ideal for vegetarians, there's always a delicious meat-free dish on the menu.

Specialities: crispy Dartmoor pork belly, home-cured gravadlax, cream teas

Sun–Thu 10–5, Fri & Sat 10–5 & 7–late

£ to ££

Parke, Bovey Tracey TQ13 9JQ
01626 830 016
www.homefarmcafe.co.uk

Getting There
The National Trust-owned Parke estate is just 3km from the Devon Expressway (A38), which connects Plymouth and Exeter, about 2km outside Bovey Tracey.

The Secret
The Sunday-afternoon music sessions here work very well, allowing you to linger over a long lunch while listening to soulful numbers by local artists.

5 SERVICE

5 HEALTHY FOOD

5 AMBIENCE

Colourful crockery, Home Farm Café

Ruby Modern Diner
Beef is the word

5

SERVICE

4

HEALTHY
FOOD

5

AMBIENCE

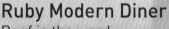

Daily 11.30–late   **££**

74 Queen Street, Exeter EX4 3RX
01392 436 168
www.rubyburgers.com

Getting There
From the city centre, walk along
Queen Street towards Exeter Central
station. The diner is on your right, by
the entrance to Northernhay Gardens.

The Secret
*If you can't decide which burger
to have, go for the sliders – three
half-size burgers of your choice
with two delicious side dishes.*

This 1950s-inspired diner offers an all-American
fast-food dining experience with a twist. All the meat,
cheese, beers and other ingredients served on site
are from West Country farms and producers. Even
the restaurant's name is inspired by a native breed of
cattle – the Red Ruby – which is supplied, in this case,
by nearby Copplestone Barton Farm.

There are more than a dozen different burgers on the
menu, as well as other exciting options, such as the
Notorious P.I.G. (pulled pork with slaw), the Turbo
Nachos (Ruby chilli with the works) and the veggie
'faloumi' burger (a falafel patty with halloumi).

A modern take on a traditional diner, this place is all
red leatherette booths and chrome mixed with rustic
wooden benches and tables.

Specialities: burgers, burgers and veggie burgers

The NoBody Inn
An epicurean's delight

5
SERVICE

4
HEALTHY FOOD

5
AMBIENCE

Mon–Sat 11–11,
Sun midday–10.30

££

Doddiscombsleigh, Exeter EX6 7PS
01647 252 394
www.nobodyinn.co.uk

Getting There
Head into Doddiscombsleigh, situated between the A30 and the A38 to the southwest of Exeter, and the pub is in the heart of the village.

The Secret
If you happen to order the last shot of a rare whisky at this pub, the empty bottle is yours to take away.

This 17th-century inn has quite a reputation among epicureans, and rightly so. The menu is imaginative and extensive, and the bar bursts with 250 wines and 250 whiskies; the whiskies range from a nip at £2.35 to a whopping £95.90 a shot.

Typical dishes include pumpkin and sage risotto and confit fillet of sea bream with a soft herb crust, creamed leeks and potatoes. The cheese platter is a great alternative to pudding – simply tick your choices on the menu, hand it over and your platter will arrive. And if you're staying overnight, try the NoBody Night Cap – a selection of nine cheeses and half a bottle of port.

The low ceilings, blackened beams and inglenook fireplace in this pub create an atmospheric backdrop.

Specialities: cheese platter, steak and NoBody ale pie

G V [icons]

Route 2
Get your kicks

As its name suggests, this café is located on Route 2 – the National Cycle Network route which, when complete, will link Kent with Cornwall. A great stop-off point on the Exeter-to-Exmouth stretch of the route, this café has seating inside and out, room to keep your gear close by and bikes to hire from the adjacent shop.

The all-day breakfast includes sausages and bacon from the local butcher, while the Green Route is a veggie fry-up and the Half Route is a smaller plate. Route 2 prides itself on using the very best local produce, and almost everything is homemade, including the ice cream and 'real Dutch apple pie'.

In the on-site bar – which is the only one in Topsham – you can sample wines from the nearby Pebblebed Vineyard, as well as Devon beer, cider and juice.

Specialities: breakfasts, ice creams, local wines

Mon–Fri 8–5,
Sat & Sun 8–6

£

1 Monmouth Hill, Topsham Hill
EX3 0JQ, 01392 875 085
www.route2topsham.co.uk

Getting There
Route 2 is on the corner of the roundabout at the bottom of Fore Street. There is a large car park opposite, on the waterfront.

The Secret
In 2014, Route 2 was named by The Guardian *as one of the top ten cycling cafés in the UK.*

5
SERVICE

5
HEALTHY FOOD

4
AMBIENCE

NORTH AFRICAN ALMOND and CITRUS CAKE £2·95

The Bakehouse
From teas to tapas

5

SERVICE

4

HEALTHY FOOD

5

AMBIENCE

Mon–Sat 9–5, also
Thu–Sat 6.30–11.30

££

3 High Street, Cullompton EX15 1AB
01884 352 22
www.thebakehousecullompton.co.uk

Getting There
This café is easy to find on the high street. There is street parking outside and a couple of car parks nearby.

The Secret
A grocer's shop in Edwardian times, this building still has the original gold-leaf lettering on the outside and meat hooks on the inside. Old photos and original brickwork adorn the café interior.

The Bakehouse is renowned for its Devon-roasted coffee, loose-leaf teas and homemade cakes. Savoury offerings include West Country-themed sharing platters and old café favourites with a modern edge. Try the Italian, a delicious toasted sandwich of salami, olives, mozzarella and tomato, and served with a pesto-mayonnaise dip. There are also soups, salads and jacket potatoes with a selection of fillings.

On Thursday, Friday and Saturday evenings, candles transform this bustling café into a sophisticated wine and tapas bar. At these times, sharing platters bursting with the flavours of Spain are typically washed down with a house cocktail or two. And, in case that wasn't enough, Wednesday nights are pizza nights, with twelve toppings to choose from.

Specialities: cakes, loose-leaf teas, tapas platters

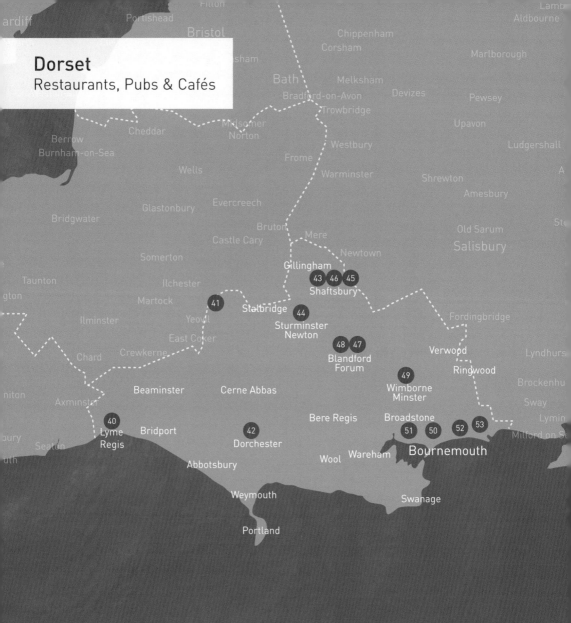

Dorset
Restaurants, Pubs & Cafés

VENUES

		page
40	Aroma	76
41	The White Post	77
42	ReLoved	78
43	The Salt Cellar	79
44	Comins Tea House	80
45	Beggars' Banquet Café	82
46	John Peel Restaurant	83
47	The Yellow Bicycle	84
48	The Dolphin	85
49	The Tickled Pig	86
50	Genève	87
51	Coast	88
52	Little Pickle	90
53	Cheese & Alfies	94

Aroma
Coffee & cake

5
SERVICE

5
HEALTHY
FOOD

5
AMBIENCE

Mon–Sat 10–4, Sun 11–4   £

6 Bridge Street, Lyme Regis
DT7 3QA, 01297 445 914
www.aromalymeregis.co.uk

Getting There
Aroma is at the bottom of town,
near to the beach (where there's
a small car park) and opposite
the Lyme Regis Museum.

The Secret
*Aroma is a brilliant place for children,
who can entertain themselves in the
'play ship' toy corner while you get
stuck into your food.*

From fry-ups and cheese on toast to pitta platters with
hummus, falafel and halloumi, Aroma produces some of
the most imaginative intolerance-friendly dishes in the
region. And just to make it really easy, all vegetarian,
vegan and gluten- and dairy-free options are clearly
marked on the menu.

Thirst-quenchers include smoothies, local ciders,
loose-leaf teas and single-origin hot chocolates. The
coffee is roasted just 12km away at The Coffee Factory
– an artisan microbrewery that responsibly sources
some of the world's best-tasting coffee.

A repository of recycled objects and down-to-earth
dishes, Aroma has distinctly laid-back, rough-around-
the-edges appeal.

Specialities: gluten-free cakes, Aroma Big Breakfast,
lime and chocolate torte

The White Post
The best of both worlds

The White Post's dual-county address has certainly had its advantages over the centuries. In days gone by, locals would exploit the different licensing hours of the two counties by carrying their pints from one end of the bar to the other to gain a little extra drinking time. Today, owner Brett Sutton celebrates his pub's quirky position by placing excellent fresh produce from both counties at the centre of the menu.

The menu manages to be ambitious without being fancy, including dishes such as salt-aged steak with black garlic and mushroom ketchup. Vegetarian options are scarce, although there are usually some seafood dishes on offer – try the barbecued mackerel with minted yoghurt and pomegranate. And if you want to make a night of it, book up one of the pub's en-suite rooms.

Specialities: Piggy Nibbles, dripping-cooked chips, Sunday lunches, six-course taster menu

Tue–Sun midday–3, Tue–Fri also 6–11, Sat also 3–11

 ££

Rimpton Hill, Yeovil BA22 8AR
01935 851 525
www.thewhitepost.com

Getting There
From the A359 between Sparkford and Yeovil, turn onto the B3148 towards Sherborne. The pub is at a small crossroads on Rimpton Hill.

The Secret
The White Post has an unusual claim to fame – it's the only pub in the UK to straddle two counties, Dorset and Somerset.

5
SERVICE

4
HEALTHY FOOD

4
AMBIENCE

ReLoved
Kitsch in the kitchen

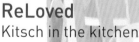
5 SERVICE

4 HEALTHY FOOD

5 AMBIENCE

Mon–Sat 9–5.30, Sun 10–4, Sat & Sun bistro 6.30–8.30   £

2 Cornhill, Dorchester DT1 1BA
01305 257 070
www.re-loved.co.uk

Getting There
The Dorchester branch of ReLoved is at the top of the pedestrianised Cornhill, opposite Lloyds bank. There is another branch at 7 North Street, Wareham.

The Secret
If you come for lunch on a Tuesday, consider staying on for Wendy's make-do-and-mend class, which comes with homemade cookies and a cuppa.

Vintage fans should make a beeline for this shop and tearoom in Dorchester. Downstairs is a lovely shop selling clothes, jewellery and retro homeware, while upstairs is this quirky tearoom – a colourful space that's decorated with some splendid kitchenware and quirkily mismatched furniture.

The staff continue the kitsch theme, dressed up to the nines in classic clobber. Even the menu has a touch of the 1950s about it, with free-range eggs, slatherings of butter and lashings of Dorset cream.

Every Friday and Saturday night, ReLoved opens as a bistro and serves such vintage-inspired dishes as homemade game cobbler and fish pie followed by ginger cake and rhubarb fool. The BYO policy adds to the frivolous atmosphere. Enjoy the old-town views.

Specialities: cream teas, knickerbocker glories

The Salt Cellar
Lunch with a view

The Salt Cellar is a popular café with panoramic views over Blackmore Vale, part of the River Stour basin. From here, on a clear day, it's possible to see as far as the Purbeck Hills in the south of the county and Glastonbury Tor in Somerset. If you want to make the most of this fantastic position by securing an outside table, it's a good idea to book ahead.

Drop by mid-morning, and you'll be in time for a coffee and toasted teacakes. A bit later, it's all about very reasonably priced, traditional, home-cooked meals, including steak and kidney pie and jacket potatoes.

Before you leave Shaftesbury, it's worth walking back around behind the café to see the historic Town Hall. This Grade II-listed building, which dates from the 19th century, is a regular site for antiques fairs.

Specialities: cream teas, sandwiches, pies, salads

Mon–Sat 9–5, Sun 10–4   £

2–4 Gold Hill Parade, Shaftesbury
SP7 8LY, 01747 851 838

Getting There
You can reach Gold Hill by walking down the cobbled lane to the side of the Town Hall, which is on Shaftesbury High Street. The Salt Cellar is behind the Town Hall.

The Secret
This café is perched at the top of one of the most famous hills in England – Gold Hill formed the backdrop to director Ridley Scott's famously nostalgic 1973 Hovis advert.

SERVICE

HEALTHY FOOD

AMBIENCE

Comins Tea House
Tea time with a difference

5
SERVICE

4
HEALTHY
FOOD

4
AMBIENCE

Wed–Sat 10–5

££

The Quarterjack, Bridge Street,
Sturminster DT10 1BZ
01258 475 389
www.cominsteahouse.co.uk

Getting There
Walk down Bridge Street in Sturminster
Newton and you'll find the elegant
Comins Tea House on your right.

The Secret
*If you're interested in the art of
tea-making, why not buy one of the
Comins tea sets for one, two or a
whole party – they make great gifts.*

Zen-like Comins Tea House offers passers-by respite
from the rush of 21st-century life. Its expert owners
– a married couple who decided to open shop after an
inspiring trip to Northern India – showcase the world's
best teas and their individual brewing methods.

The range of single-estate teas on offer here is mind-
boggling. Sample a pot of the light Japanese green
tea, which comes with a thermos holding enough hot
water for four refills, as well as a clever timer system
that promises a perfectly brewed cup each time.

While you're sipping away, try the homemade *gyoza*
(dainty Japanese dumplings), served with chilli and
soy dipping sauces. Afterwards, treat yourself to a
slice of what's likely to be the most delicious teabread
you've ever tasted.

Specialities: single-estate teas, *gyoza*, teabread

Beggars' Banquet Café
The world on a plate

5 SERVICE

5 HEALTHY FOOD

4 AMBIENCE

Mon–Sat 9–5,
Fri & Sat also 7–9

£££

Mustons Lane, Shaftesbury
SP7 8AD, 01747 850 332
www.beggarsbanquetcafe.co.uk

Getting There
From Shaftesbury High Street, turn onto Mustons Lane and you'll find the café in a private courtyard.

The Secret
This café has a pop-up stall at the small, family-friendly Larmer Tree Festival – an annual summer music event at Larmer Tree Gardens on the Wiltshire/Dorset border.

Beggars' Banquet Café is approached via a gravel courtyard that's scattered with tables and pretty parasols. Leading off the yard is the interesting café interior, its walls decorated with rare and vintage records. On the opposite side of the yard is a fairy light-festooned cocktail lounge, which holds regular live-music nights.

The vegetarian and vegan dishes here are truly international, with everything from chilli-bean and cheese burritos to veggie moussaka, miso soup and Thai 'no-fish' cakes. The homemade spelt bread, flourless chocolate and almond cake, brownies and flapjacks are particularly enticing. Many of these sweet treats are vegan, as well as gluten- and dairy-free.

Beggars' Banquet promises some serious gastronomic globetrotting, while using the freshest local ingredients.

Specialities: falafel burgers, Mediterranean breakfasts

OUR ALL-DAY BREAKFASTS

ALL COME WITH A DRINK UP TO THE VALUE OF £1.90

THE B.I.G - £8.95
2 TOAST, 2 EGGS, 3 BACON, 3 SAUSAGE, 3 HASH BROWNS, BEANS & TOMATOES

THE PEEL - £7.95
2 TOAST, 2 EGGS, 2 BACON, 2 SAUSAGE, BEANS & HASH BROWNS OR TOMATOES

STANDARD - £5.70
1 TOAST, 1 EGG, 2 BACON, 1 SAUSAGE, BEANS, TOMATOES OR A BIT OF BOTH (OR 2 FOR £11.00)

John Peel Restaurant
Greatness is a greasy spoon

For those of us old enough to have had a favourite greasy spoon as a child, eating at the John Peel Restaurant is like stepping back in time – you're guaranteed a warm welcome, a decent mug of tea and a hearty fry-up. The manager greets his regulars by name, which is a pleasure to witness.

The interior is of the old-school caff variety – no-frills, but spotlessly clean – and the menu features down-to-earth dishes, including some all-day breakfast specials.

This café is a Shaftesbury institution, with an army of loyal patrons who wouldn't miss out on their weekend fry-up for love nor money. Despite its name, it has nothing to do with the well-known BBC Radio 1 DJ.

Be warned: weekends get very busy, so arrive early.

Speciality: the Peel Breakfast

Mon–Sat 8–6, Sun 9–5.30 £

52 High Street, Shaftesbury SP7 8AA
01747 853 178

Getting There
The restaurant is found on the High Street (B3091) in Shaftesbury, just past the junction with Mustons Lane. From here, it's just a 2-minute walk to well-known Gold Hill.

The Secret
The Peel Breakfast – a colossal fry-up that can hardly fit on the plate – is said to be one of the best hangover cures in the southwest.

5 SERVICE

3 HEALTHY FOOD

3 AMBIENCE

The Yellow Bicycle
Flatbread fun

(5) **SERVICE**

(4) **HEALTHY FOOD**

(3) **AMBIENCE**

Tue–Sat 8.30–5, call for details of supper evenings £

30a Salisbury Street, Blandford Forum DT11 7AR, 01258 480 356
www.facebook.com/yellowbicyclecafe

Getting There
This café can be found part way up Salisbury Street on the right-hand side, just before the junction to the pretty street known as The Plocks.

The Secret
This café loves to make its customers feel part of its lively community. Photo competitions involving yellow bikes and silly poses have been known!

The Yellow Bicycle is an ideal place to take little ones for a treat. The interior is modern and fun, decked out mainly in muted greys, except for the yellow bicycle that hangs on the wall and the bright crockery to match.

Every morning, a giant batch of fresh sourdough is prepared to accommodate the dozens of flatbread-pizza orders made throughout the day. The chorizo, rocket and sundried-tomato combination is particularly good. Also on offer are delicious homemade cakes, including a gigantic chocolate creation adorned with chocolate butter cream and chocolate buttons and fingers. A freshly made filter coffee is the perfect accompaniment.

This restaurant hosts set-menu supper evenings, usually on an ad-hoc basis in the low season, on the last Saturday of the month. Call ahead for details.

Specialities: flatbread pizzas, cakes, coffee

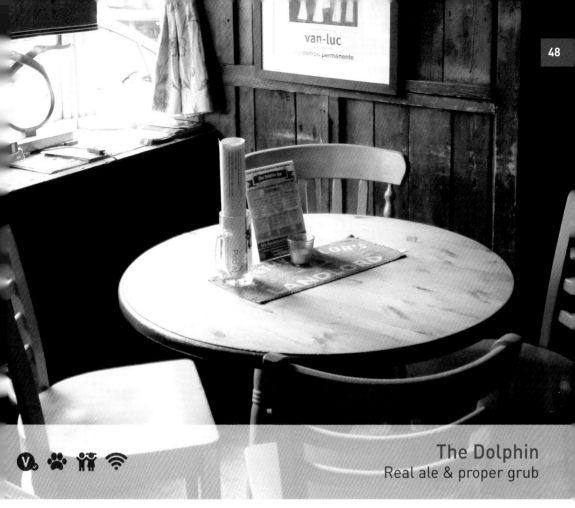

The Dolphin
Real ale & proper grub

Rebuilt following the Great Fire of Blandford Forum in 1731, which devastated much of the town, The Dolphin weighs heavy with history and intrigue. Legend has it the pub is haunted by a shawl-clad young woman, whose burnt face is revealed on being approached.

The Dolphin offers traditional pub grub, with old favourites such as ham, egg and chips and sticky-toffee pudding with custard. Keep an eye out for the cutlery symbol on the menu, which suggests the best beer to pair with different dishes. While you're eating, be sure to take a look at the works by local artists on the walls.

This real-ale pub is ideal for people with dogs. You can even treat the hound to a portion of Man's Best Friend – a bowl of prime meaty chunks in gravy with a garnish of 'the finest doggy biscuits'.

Specialities: the 42 Mix Grill, steak and Jimmy pie

Mon–Sat midday–3 & 6–9, Sun midday–6   ££

42 East Street, Blandford Forum DT11 7DR, 01258 456 813 www.thedolphinblandford.co.uk

Getting There
The Dolphin is easily found on East Street (B3082), opposite Common Lane. There is plenty of street parking and car parks close by.

The Secret
Expect great-tasting beers with names such as 'Slasher' and 'Jimmy' at this CAMRA pub, part of the Piddle Brewery group.

4
SERVICE

3
HEALTHY FOOD

3
AMBIENCE

The Tickled Pig
Good-life gastronomy

4

SERVICE

4

HEALTHY FOOD

4

AMBIENCE

Daily midday–2.30 & 7–9, Sat from 10, closed Sun eve

££

26 West Borough, Wimborne
BH21 1NF, 01202 886 778
www.thetickledpig.co.uk

Getting There
The Tickled Pig is on West Borough (B3078), a few doors up from the junction with Priors Walk (B3078).

The Secret
As well as fantastic home-reared organic food in the restaurant, The Tickled Pig offers cookery courses in everything from bread-making to cooking fish. Lunch is often included.

The sustainable-food philosophy at The Tickled Pig is summed up by the mantra, 'taking food back to its roots'. Expect the highest-quality ingredients, almost all of which are local, seasonal and organic. The kitchen garden supplies all vegetables, salad and herbs used in the restaurant, while Oxford Sandy and Black pigs are bred by the team for pork.

Dishes are classic yet creative, such as hot-smoked brisket with spicy slaw and smashed new potatoes, pork belly with burnt-apple and vanilla puree, and Purbeck crab with saffron and garlic mayonnaise.

The restaurant, which occupies an old shop in the centre of the market town of Wimborne, has a lovely terrace at the rear. There's also an on-site deli, with wall-to-wall charcuterie, pickles, cheeses and more.

Specialities: slow-roast pork belly, chips, scallops

Genève
Smoke & sauce

From the moment you arrive at Genève, you're treated like one of the family. This cool restaurant's low-lit interior has attractive, exposed-brick walls and a lively open kitchen, which allows for a little drama.

The menu is about quality rather than quantity, and, as you'd expect from an American-style diner, it's big on meat. Try the umami burger, which comes piled high with shiitake mushrooms, pickled coleslaw and watercress. Another must-taste is the 18-hour hickory-infused pulled pork, which comes with a dash of magic in the shape of the chef's own BBQ sauce. This mouthwatering concoction is unlike anything you can buy bottled.

All ingredients are locally sourced and all dishes are made from scratch – even the southern-style meat dishes, thanks to the on-site smoker.

Specialities: umami burger, chef's own BBQ Sauce

Tue–Sat midday-3 & 6-10   ££

128 Poole Road, Westbourne,
Bournemouth BH4 9EF
01202 768 864
www.geneveeatery.co.uk

Getting There
Turn off the A35 as it joins the A338, and make your way onto Poole Road. There is plenty of street parking if you're driving.

The Secret
Are you brave enough to take on the Wings Heat Challenge? It involves eating chicken wings that come with a sauce so hot it's applied with a pipette!

5
SERVICE

4
HEALTHY FOOD

3
AMBIENCE

Coffee Shop **Coast** Surf S.

Coast
Surf, ride, skate & coffee

4

SERVICE

4

HEALTHY FOOD

3

AMBIENCE

Mon–Sat 9–5, Sun 10–4   £

91 Salterns Road, Poole BH14 8BL
01202 732 100
www.wearecoast.com

Getting There
Turn off the A35 onto Salterns Road, and Coast is at the end of the road on the left-hand side. There are a handful of parking spaces right outside the shop.

The Secret
This café hosts a series of popular events, from gatherings to swap pre-loved surf equipment to screenings of extreme sports-themed films.

As part of a surfing, cycling and skating shop, this laid-back, buzzing café is a draw for those who love extreme sports and great coffee. With surfboards suspended from the ceiling and funky artworks on the walls, it certainly feels like the place to be in Poole.

The menu might be limited, but it's good. Enjoy a freshly made roll, panini or slice of cake with a mug of fresh coffee. Be warned: the BLTs are a dangerous combination of irresistible and immense.

The minimalist interior of the café is airy and spacious, and bathed in a warm, natural light. There are fewer tables than could feasibly be crammed in, which is part of its appeal. So, after kitting yourself out in the shop with everything you need for some adrenalin-fuelled fun, simply sit back and enjoy the vibe.

Specialities: BLTs, coffee, cakes

Little Pickle
Cute overload

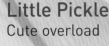

5 SERVICE

5 HEALTHY FOOD

4 AMBIENCE

Mon–Sat 9–4.30 £

737 Christchurch Road, Boscombe
BH7 6AQ, 01202 900 899
www.littlepickledelicafe.co.uk

Getting There
Little Pickle is at the junction of Chessel
Avenue on Christchurch Road (A35).
You'll find plenty of street parking on
Chessel Avenue.

The Secret
*You can order a picnic hamper from
this cosy little café – it will contain
every bit of grub you could possibly
need for a day at the beach.*

Everything about Little Pickle is cute. From its name
to its shabby-chic décor, this café is an oasis amid the
hustle and bustle of Boscombe's busy town centre.

The menu is simple yet fun, ranging from dippy boiled
eggs to the Ultimate Fish Finger Sarnie. This doorstop
of a ciabatta sandwich, jam-packed with fish fingers,
salad, ketchup and mayonnaise, is a perfect grown-
up version of an enduring childhood favourite. The
house veggie burger is a courgette fritter with grilled
mushrooms and aubergine, avocado or chilli salsa, and
skinny chips. There are also lots of sharing options on
offer here, including the Dorset deli board and the basic
but brilliant bucket of chips.

The BYO late-night supper evenings, which take place
on the last Thursday of each month, book up fast.

Speciality: the Ultimate Fish Finger Sarnie

Fresh herbs, Little Pickle

Cheese & Alfies
Eggs every way

5
SERVICE

4
HEALTHY FOOD

5
AMBIENCE

Mon & Tue 8.30–5, Wed–Fri/
Sat/Sun 8.30–9.30/8.30/4   **£**

10 Church Street, Christchurch
BH23 1BW, 01202 487 000
www.cheeseandalfies.com

Getting There
You can find Cheese & Alfies in the
centre of Christchurch, just a stone's
throw from Christchurch Priory.

The Secret
*Cheese & Alfies offers cookery
classes on a Monday night. These
involve preparing a three-course
meal (two dishes per course) with
the head chef, Daff. Wine is included.*

The breakfast menu at this cool café devotes an entire
section to the humble egg, in all its free-range glory.
Choose between Benedict, Blackstone, Florentine,
Royale and even the good old, soft-boiled sort, complete
with a battery of buttered soldiers. For something more
filling, try the traditional full English, served sizzling in
a cast-iron skillet, and for something sweeter, try the
pancakes and homemade brioche French toast.

But it's not all about breakfast at Cheese & Alfies.
There's also an evening menu, which includes some
great creations. Try the goat's cheese and sweet-potato
risotto or the roasted loin of cod with sautéed potatoes,
spinach and Spanish-style dressing. For a group of
meat-lovers, the Infamous Big Brother Sharer (four
burgers in one) is perfect.

Specialities: eggy breakfasts, burgers

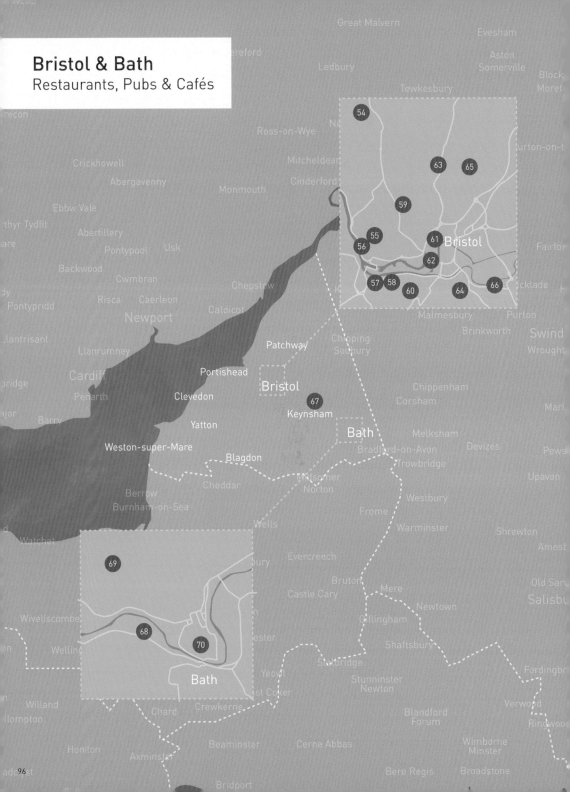

Bristol & Bath
Restaurants, Pubs & Cafés

VENUES

		page
54	Venue 35	98
55	The Clifton Sausage	99
56	Wallfish Bistro	100
57	The Thali Café	102
58	Soukitchen	104
59	Yume Kitchen	105
60	The Old Bookshop	106
61	Full Court Press	107
62	Mud Dock	108
63	Café Ronak	110
64	Historical Dining Rooms	111
65	St Werburghs City Farm Café	112
66	The Tube Diner	114
67	Pomegranate Café Restaurant	118
68	Burgers and Barrels	119
69	The Bath Priory	120
70	Chapel Arts Centre Café	122

Venue 35
Breakfast in bread

5 SERVICE

4 HEALTHY FOOD

4 AMBIENCE

Mon 9–5, Tue–Sat 9–6, Sun 10–4   ££

135 Stoke Lane, Westbury-on-Trym, Bristol BS9 3RW, 0117 329 0443
www.venue35.co.uk

Getting There
This ever-popular Bristol café is on Stoke Lane, next door to the Co-operative supermarket. There is plenty of street parking close by.

The Secret
Venue 35 offers what has to be the most comprehensive gluten-free menu in the city, which includes versions of many of its flagship dishes.

This café bar has one of the most extensive menus we've seen. Choose from the long list of big breakfasts (you get a free hot drink before 11am), light lunches and more robust dishes, such as bangers and mash, burger and chips, and spaghetti bolognese.

But the real event of the week is Sunday lunch, which attracts people from across the city. West Country beef is usually one of the meat options, although sometimes the kitchen puts on one of its fabled hog roasts, which yield 10-hour slow-roasted pork that really does melt in the mouth.

Venue 35 attracts families, thanks to its all-day food service, versatile menu and spacious layout, which allows for buggies. There's also a dedicated play area to keep toddlers occupied while you enjoy your food.

Specialities: breakfasts, nachos, Cajun-chicken salad

The Clifton Sausage
Mad about pub grub

The Clifton Sausage, just a stone's throw from the green expanse of Clifton Down, aims to put traditional British food back on the map. As its name suggests, this restaurant offers an impressive array of sausages, including the Clifton, which combines pork, wholegrain mustard and cider to mouthwatering effect. Tuck in with either mash or champ and lashings of onion gravy.

There's also a homemade vegetarian sausage on offer here, and many sausage-free meals to choose from. The pork belly, served with roasted sweet-potato mash, summer cabbage, apple sauce, cider gravy and crackling, is as good as it sounds.

If you're just popping in for a drink, then a bar snack is definitely in order – the homemade sausage rolls with Colman's mustard are delicious.

Speciality: sausages (pork and vegetarian)

Daily midday–midnight ££

7 Portland Street, Bristol BS8 4JA
0117 973 1192
www.cliftonsausage.co.uk

Getting There
The Clifton Sausage is on the corner of Waterloo Street and Portland Street in the heart of Clifton Village, a very pretty and fashionable area of Bristol.

The Secret
The Clifton Sausage uses free-range pork from Gloucester Old Spot pigs, which does a lot to explain their excellent quality and great taste.

 5 SERVICE

 4 HEALTHY FOOD

 5 AMBIENCE

Wallfish Bistro
Sunday salvation

5
SERVICE

5
HEALTHY
FOOD

5
AMBIENCE

Wed–Sat/Sun midday–3 & 6–10/9, Sat & Sun brunch 10–3 **££**

112 Princess Victoria Street, Bristol
BS8 4DB, 0117 973 5435
www.wallfishbistro.co.uk

Getting There
This restaurant is at the western end of Princess Victoria Street, near the southern end of Clifton Down.

The Secret
This bistro occupies the site where the late Keith Floyd had his first business, from 1969 to 1972. And, with its no-fuss approach and big flavours, the chef would surely have approved.

Any restaurant that serves brunch cocktails is worth noting, but if it also serves great-quality ingredients in creative combinations, you know you're onto something special. The Wallfish Bistro is just such a place.

The non-liquid items on the brunch menu here can only be described as posh fry-ups – each item has a stylish twist to make it stand out. Take the smoked salmon and poached egg, which comes with chive butter, or the boiled egg and soldiers, which is served with celery salt. They're small additions, maybe, but they add a sophisticated dimension to otherwise classic dishes.

There are also lunch and supper menus, which are just as understated and satisfying as brunch. BYO Wednesdays are a popular, relaxed affair.

Specialities: Portland oysters, lobster risotto, Bloody Marys

The Thali Café
Time for tiffin

5 SERVICE

5 HEALTHY FOOD

5 AMBIENCE

Daily midday–late

££

Tobacco Factory, North Street,
Bristol BS3 1TF, 0117 953 2783
www.thethalicafe.co.uk

Getting There
The Southville branch of this café
is easily located on North Street
(B3120), in the old Tobacco Factory.
There is street parking close by.

The Secret
*The Thali Café has been known to raise
large sums for great environmental
and social causes, including more than
£10,000 for safe water in rural India.*

This restaurant is bright, cheery and ever so slightly
kitsch – it will probably come as no surprise that the
team here started off selling street food at festivals.
Now a thriving brand, Thali has five branches in Bristol,
this one in Southville being the biggest.

Expect healthy, beautifully presented modern Indian
food served on thali plates – traditionally moulded metal
plates with compartments for separate mini-dishes.
Menu items are marked with a D, V or G to indicate
dairy-free, vegetarian and gluten-free, respectively.

Thali has robust ethical credentials, sourcing most of
its ingredients within a 30km radius of the city. All meat
and eggs are free-range and all dairy is organic. In fact,
Thali is so green, it's received the highest three-star
rating from the Sustainable Restaurant Association.

Speciality: modern vegetarian Indian food

Soukitchen
The magic of Marrakech

5
SERVICE

5
HEALTHY
FOOD

4
AMBIENCE

Mon–Fri midday–3 & 6–10,
Sat/Sun 10–3 & 6–10/9   ££

277 North Street, Bedminster,
Bristol BS3 1JP, 0117 966 6880
www.soukitchen.co.uk

Getting There
Soukitchen sits on the corner
of North Street and Raleigh
Road in Bedminster, opposite
the Tobacco Factory.

The Secret
*This café has its own brand of
exotic ingredients for sale. Take a
moment to admire the beautiful
label designs before tucking in.*

Soukitchen is the place to go for an authentic taste
of Middle Eastern market and street food. Expect
traditional dishes from the region – everything from
crisp, hot falafels straight from the fryer to delicately
spiced tagines – alongside some little-known dishes
that balance out the menu.

The food of the Middle East tends to be fairly healthy,
making clever use of herbs and spices rather than
refined sugars and bad fats to bring dishes to life.
The food here is no exception.

Soukitchen's colourful interior features large, mosaic-
like patterns on the walls and jars of ingredients lining
the shelves. The fun crockery and £10 lunch platters
add to its appeal.

Specialities: kebabs, homemade baklava, shakshouka

Yume Kitchen
A dream kitchen

The name Yume may sound like a clever play on words, but it actually means 'dream' in Japanese. And, in the case of this authentic independent sushi bar – which blows better-known fast-food sushi chains out of the water – the food really does live up to the name.

The deftly executed, subtly flavoured sushi and sashimi platters, arranged attractively on slabs of slate, are popular choices. But if you're after something more substantial, the katsu curry, yakisoba noodles and sweet-soy glazed chicken teriyaki are all great options. The meat is all higher-welfare, and the fish is bought fresh every morning, to ensure the highest quality.

As you might expect, Bristol's first Japanese-owned restaurant has a real following among die-hard fans of the country's culture and cuisine.

Specialities: sushi, miso soup, katsu curry

Sun–Thu midday–9.30,
Fri & Sat midday–10.30
££

9 Cotham Hill, Bristol BS6 6LD
0117 200 2888
www.yumekitchen.co.uk

Getting There
Heading north on Whiteladies Road (A4018), turn right onto Cotham Hill and Yume is on the right-hand side.

The Secret
No Japanese meal would be complete without some nihonshu *(sake); if you ask the staff, you'll receive a quick lesson in the proper way of pouring it.*

4
SERVICE

5
HEALTHY
FOOD

3
AMBIENCE

The Old Bookshop
Food for sharing

SERVICE 4

HEALTHY FOOD 4

AMBIENCE 4

Mon 5–11, Tue–Sat
10.30–11, Sun 11.30–11   £

65 North Street, Bristol BS3 1ES
0117 953 5222
www.theoldbookshop.co.uk

Getting There
The Old Bookshop is located between
Bedminster and Southville, on busy
North Street. There is plenty of street
parking in the area.

The Secret
*This café opens its doors to guest
chefs, pop-up outfits and street-food
vendors – an innovative feature that
makes for an ever-changing menu.*

On a quiet afternoon, this curio-packed café is the
perfect place to meet up with friends or settle down
with a pint and a good book. Come the evening, it's
transformed into a vibrant hangout and, at times,
live-music venue.

The menu has enough variety to keep everyone happy,
thanks to its focus on Spanish-inspired tapas dishes.
But for anyone who prefers to keep their food to
themselves, there are larger dishes to choose from.
Eat out in the garden if you can get a table.

The Old Bookshop is certainly eccentric – its walls
are decked out with everything from stuffed animals
to musical instruments – but it's undeniably warm
and welcoming. Never more so, in fact, than at one
of its cosy open-mic or movie nights in winter.

Specialities: sweet-chilli fishcakes, lamb kebabs

Full Court Press
Cool beans!

A brew from this speciality coffee house, which puts the humble coffee bean at the centre of everything it does, couldn't be further from the bog-standard high-street coffee most of us knock back on a daily basis.

Here, every step of the journey to bring you your chosen cup of coffee has been perfected, from the brewing technique to the temperature of the milk served alongside. It's like a wine-tasting experience, only for lovers of the brown stuff.

Interestingly, staff advise against adding sugar to their blends, which are brewed to be exceptionally smooth and devoid of acrid hints – there isn't a sugar bowl in sight.

For those who have a serious coffee habit, courses are available, from filter brewing to barista skills.

Speciality: coffee, coffee and more coffee

Mon–Fri 7.30–5, Sat 9–5, Sun 10–4

£

59 Broad Street, Bristol BS1 2EJ
07794 808 552
www.fcpcoffee.com

Getting There
This coffee house is right next door to The Grand Hotel on Broad Street, just a short walk from food-focused St Nicholas Market (see p243).

The Secret
The name of this coffee house refers to a no-compromise, all-out move in basketball, which sums up the team's approach to quality and service.

5
SERVICE

4
HEALTHY FOOD

4
AMBIENCE

Mud Dock
Bikes, boats & Bloody Marys

5
SERVICE

4
HEALTHY
FOOD

5
AMBIENCE

Mon 9.30–5, Tue–Fri
9.30–10, Sat 9–10, Sun 9–5   **££**

40 The Grove, Bristol BS1 4RB
0117 934 9734
www.mud-dock.co.uk

Getting There
You'll find Mud Dock – a large
renovated warehouse next to the
river – a couple of minutes' walk
south from regal Queen Square.

The Secret
*The on-site Bike Shed offers lockers,
showers and changing facilities for a
day (£2), a week (£10), a month (£30) or
more. Great if you're staying in the area.*

Mud Dock, with its big downstairs bike shop and cool
upstairs café, is a nerve centre for Bristol cyclists, who
come here to buy bikes, components and accessories,
mend their kit, hone their skills in bike maintenance
and break up long rides with a coffee, lunch or beer.

Situated right on the city's floating harbour in an old
and imposing redbrick warehouse, Mud Dock offers a
rather unique space that makes a virtue of its industrial
heritage. Huge windows let light flood into the dining
area, which spills out onto a roof terrace overlooking
narrow boats on the river. Elsewhere, chunky chains,
metal surfaces and wooden furniture decorate the
interior, in keeping with the building's low-tech style.

The menu is fantastic and brunches at weekends come
with a Bloody Mary – great for anyone with a sore head.

Specialities: Mud Dock mezze, sandwiches, salads

Café Ronak
The secret garden

5
SERVICE

5
HEALTHY FOOD

5
AMBIENCE

Mon–Sat 7–6, Sun 9–5 £

169 Gloucester Road, Bristol
BS7 8BE, 0117 307 0392
www.caferonak.co.uk

Getting There
Look out for the café's red awning and covered seating on Gloucester Road (A38), next to the Tesco Express.

The Secret
Despite its Persian food, this café is – in all other ways – a shrine to the local area. It displays local art, hosts local musicians, uses 90% local produce and has a loyal band of local followers.

From its outstanding coffee and specialist teas to its internationally inspired food and exemplary service, Café Ronak – which takes its name from the Farsi word for 'light' – gets it right again and again.

The menu, which is known for its ethically sourced ingredients, caters to vegans, hardened carnivores and everyone in between. If you're in need of a pick-me-up rather than full-blown meal, try the homemade baklava with your coffee or a summer smoothie.

On a nice day, take a seat in the back garden under the leafy canopy; if you get chilly, wrap up in one of the blankets that are dotted around. Otherwise, grab a table inside the café, where the Middle Eastern colours and textures provide a refreshing contrast to the shabby-chic style that defines so many cafés these days.

Specialities: coffee, smoothies, breakfasts

Historical Dining Rooms
History is served!

The minute you enter the Historical Dining Rooms – via a rather anonymous street-level side door and up a flight of stairs, where you ring a butler's bell to gain access – you genuinely feel as though you're stepping into another era. The 26-seat, Regency-style dining room has parquet flooring, dark-wood panelling, mint-green walls and all kinds of historical artefacts, from heavy-framed paintings to heritage rugs.

And that's before you even glance at the menus – or 'bills of fare', as they're known – with their evocatively named dishes. Try the 'cottage pye and rost beef' or the 'rabbit; buttered, roasted, potted, preserved', which is served with potted umbles (offal), smoked lard and horse parsley. To create these, the chefs draw on written accounts of royal banquets dating back as far as 1390. All menu items include the original date and creator.

Specialities: rare-breed Sunday roasts, veal sweetbreads

Wed–Sat 6–9.30,
Sun midday–4

££

The Black Door, Windsor Terrace,
Bristol BS3 4RY, 0117 972 0366
www.historical-dining-rooms.co.uk

Getting There
This pub is located on the St Luke's Road end of Windsor Terrace, a short walk away from Victoria Park.

The Secret
For anyone who wants to try some heritage food with a lighter touch, eat at the Star and Dove, the pub beneath the restaurant. The two outfits share the same historically curious chefs.

5

SERVICE

4

HEALTHY
FOOD

5

AMBIENCE

St Werburghs City Farm Café
A rural retreat

5

SERVICE

5

HEALTHY
FOOD

4

AMBIENCE

Summer Wed–Mon 10–5,
winter Wed–Mon 10–4

£

Watercress Road, Bristol BS2 9YJ
0117 908 0798
www.swcityfarm.co.uk/animals

Getting There
On Mina Road, look out for signs
to the farm. Park wherever you can
and the café is past the farm on the right.

The Secret
*St Werburghs is a social enterprise as
much as it is a farm, with volunteering
programmes and community events.
Local allotment holders can even swap
spare veg for something in the café.*

The journey to St Werburghs City Farm is quite surreal.
One minute, you're driving through suburban Bristol,
the next, you're passing some colourful and very quirky
houses. At this point, prepare yourself for something
rather special just around the corner – a Hobbit-like
building containing St Werburghs City Farm Café.

This farm may be tiny by rural standards, but it
produces an impressive amount of meat, eggs and
vegetables, which get star billing on the café menu.
Expect farm-reared mutton, lamb, goat, pork, venison
and even wild rabbit, as well as lots of fresh produce.

No visit to the café would be complete without meeting
the pigs, goats, chickens and ducks who live here or
– for families – a trip to the adventure playground.

Specialities: sausages, foraged greens, homegrown
produce

The Tube Diner
Burgers & banquettes

5
SERVICE

4
HEALTHY
FOOD

5
AMBIENCE

Mon–Fri 8–4, Sat 9–3,
also Fri & Sat 6–9

££

Paintworks, Bath Road,
Bristol BS4 3EH
07949 694 979
www.thetubediner.co.uk

Getting There
Turn into the Paintworks complex
from Bath Road and follow the road –
you can't miss the two silver caravans
on the right-hand side!

The Secret
*Atmospheric and unusual, the Tube
Diner can be hired for parties and
other gatherings. Call for details.*

Picture two silver American Airstream caravans, one
containing a kitchen, the other a 1950s diner, and you'll
get a sense of the retro vibe at this café in the heart
of Bristol's creative quarter. With their innovative feel,
these vans make even Astroturf look cool.

The team behind The Tube Diner wanted to create a
café that stood out, and boy did they succeed. They
considered plane fuselages, old school buses and even
a grain silo as possible housing for their new venture,
before settling on the Airstreams.

When dining here, surrounded by red leatherette,
chrome, and black and white floor tiles, it's easy to
forget you're in contemporary Bristol. The kitchen
excels at fresh, fast food, including burgers made
with minced steak from a local Somerset butcher.

Specialities: short-stack American pancakes, burgers

Herb oil, Pomegranate Café Restaurant

Pomegranate Café Restaurant
Mediterranean magic

5
SERVICE

5
HEALTHY
FOOD

5
AMBIENCE

Mon–Fri 8–2.30, Sat 9–2.30, also Thu–Sat 6–9 £

19 Temple Street, Keynsham, Bristol BS31 1HF
0117 986 4888

Getting There
Keynsham is midway between Bristol and Bath on the A4; Pomegranate is at the southern end of the High Street.

The Secret
Pomegranate has a salad bar and deli counter with nibbles to mix and match, including sun-dried tomatoes, stuffed vine leaves and homemade coleslaw; eat in or take away.

Café by day, restaurant by night, Pomegranate might not look very exciting from the outside, but don't be fooled – the food and service here are outstanding.

Firstly, it would be a challenge to find a better breakfast in the area than the one served here. Generous portions, fantastic ingredients and service with a smile will have you plotting your next visit before you've even finished your eggs. And then there's lunch, which takes on a distinctly Mediterranean flavour, with dishes such as stuffed, baked aubergine, grilled halloumi and antipasti platters. The team's passion for beautifully cooked, high-quality dishes is evident in every plate.

The other crucial piece of information to impart is that Pomegranate has a BYO service with free corkage, so come armed with a bottle.

Specialities: cooked breakfasts, lamb shanks, steaks

Burgers and Barrels
Mouthwatering meat

Burgers and Barrels serves up food that just demands to be eaten. Its burgers come piled high with juicy meat and are topped with all manner of mouthwatering extras; take the Immortal burger, which comes layered with sautéed mushrooms, blue cheese and an onion confit that will leave you in a daze of tasty contentment.

Cocktails are made from scratch at the bar by mixing maestros Ronnie, Ahmed and their team. These are the perfect diversion when waiting to be seated, and do a great job of washing down all that delicious stodge when the time comes to eat.

It can get busy here, despite stools at the bar and tables on the pavement outside. But it's this snug size that guarantees a bustling, intimate atmosphere at pretty much any time of day. The service is superb.

Specialities: Immortal burger, cranberry and lychee juice

Mon–Thu midday–10, Fri & Sat midday–11, Sun 1–9   ££

2 Victoria Buildings, Lower Bristol Road, Bath BA2 3EH, 01225 313 030
www.burgersnbarrels.co.uk

Getting There
This restaurant is just outside Bath city centre, on the main road to Bristol (A36), right next to the traffic lights at the junction of the B3111.

The Secret
Evening high jinks are routine here, from happy hours and pub quizzes to The Hulk Challenge – a mission to devour 2kg of burger in 30 minutes.

5
SERVICE

4
HEALTHY FOOD

3
AMBIENCE

The Bath Priory
A very English affair

5

SERVICE

5

HEALTHY
FOOD

5

AMBIENCE

Daily 12.30–2.30, 3–4.30
& 6.30–9.30   **£££**

Weston Road, Bath BA1 2XT
01225 331 922
www.thebathpriory.co.uk

Getting There
From Weston Road, northwest of
Bath city centre, turn left into the
private gravelled car park, just before
the road becomes Weston Lane.

The Secret
*If you really want to push the boat
out, book yourself in for a treatment
at the on-site Garden Spa. Spa days
and breaks are also on offer.*

Enjoying the delightful English ritual of afternoon tea at
Bath Priory has to be one of the most luxurious treats
on offer in the southwest. Have it on the lawn or beside
a crackling log fire, depending on the season.

This exciting daily event features a tiered platter of
delicate sandwiches and homemade cakes, biscuits
and oven-warm scones with lashings of West Country
clotted cream and preserves. Served with your choice
of tea or coffee, or even a glass of Perrier-Jouët
Champagne, it is completely and utterly decadent.

As afternoon blends into evening, it's all about the
on-site Michelin-starred restaurant – if you're feeling
flush, that is. The seven-course tasting menu here is
exquisite, but then so is everything else on the menu.
Work up an appetite with a walk around the city first.

Specialities: afternoon tea, seven-course tasting menu

Chapel Arts Centre Café
Veggie heaven

5
SERVICE

5
HEALTHY
FOOD

5
AMBIENCE

Mon–Sat 9–5.30,
Sun 10–4

£

St James Memorial Hall, Lower
Borough Walls, Bath BA1 1QR
01225 920 256
www.chapelarts.org/chapel_arts/cafe

Getting There
Head down the steps of the Chapel
Arts Centre to the basement, where
you'll find this sweet little café.

The Secret
*The arts centre above the café is
considered to be Bath's foremost
alternative-arts centre, hosting
everything from comedy to mime.*

Everything is homemade at Chapel Arts Centre Café,
and it shows. This popular place is known for its entirely
vegetarian menu, especially its moreish, made-to-order
flatbreads, which make for a perfect pre-show snack.

Try the Farmer, which combines homemade tomato
sauce, roasted red onions, peppers, goats' cheese,
spring onions, sweetcorn and pesto on a delicate
flatbread. Another favourite is the Breakfast, made
with a fried egg, cherry tomatoes, garlic mushrooms,
baked beans, onion marmalade, and – of course – a
flatbread. The cakes and pastries are also delicious,
thanks to the French owner's baking background.

The café doubles up as a gallery space displaying local
art, so try to drag your eyes away from your flavour-
packed feast from time to time to take it all in.

Specialities: flatbreads, salads, cakes

Somerset
Restaurants, Pubs & Cafés

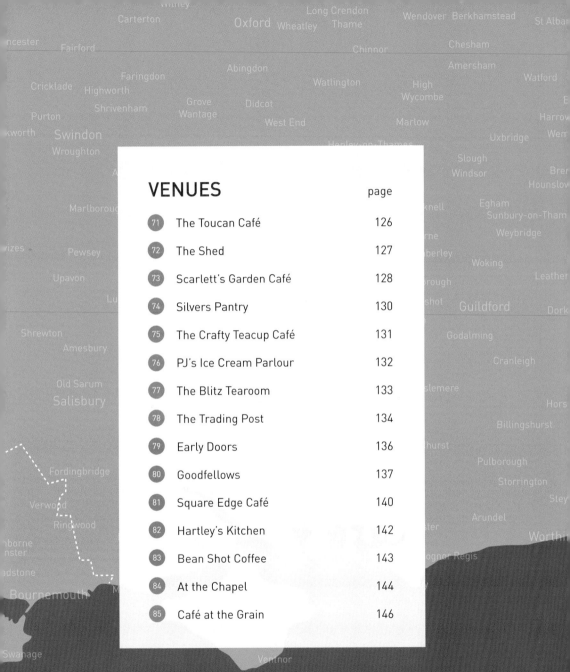

VENUES

		page
71	The Toucan Café	126
72	The Shed	127
73	Scarlett's Garden Café	128
74	Silvers Pantry	130
75	The Crafty Teacup Café	131
76	PJ's Ice Cream Parlour	132
77	The Blitz Tearoom	133
78	The Trading Post	134
79	Early Doors	136
80	Goodfellows	137
81	Square Edge Café	140
82	Hartley's Kitchen	142
83	Bean Shot Coffee	143
84	At the Chapel	144
85	Café at the Grain	146

The Toucan Café
Holistic & happy

5
SERVICE

5
HEALTHY FOOD

5
AMBIENCE

Summer Mon–Sat 8.30–5, winter Mon–Sat 8.30–4.30 **£**

3 The Parade, Minehead TA24 5NL
01643 706 101
www.toucanwholefoods.co.uk

Getting There
Toucan Wholefoods and its on-site café can be found on The Parade in the heart of Minehead, next door to Barclays bank.

The Secret
If you can't get enough of the Toucan Café's heavenly health food, you can make use of its excellent takeaway and outside catering services.

The menu at this vegetarian café has a strong emphasis on local, seasonal and organic produce. It includes both light and substantial options, from meze platters and superfood salads to the show-stealing McToucan burger – a kidney-bean patty spiced with garlic, ginger, cumin, coriander, paprika and a kick of chilli. There are lots of gluten-free and vegan choices on offer, as well as organic coffee, teas, smoothies, cakes and bakes.

The café has four rooms to choose between: the bright main room, the Moroccan-themed lounge, the art room, which displays works by local artists, and the snug. Dogs are welcome in all. On the floor above the café is a complementary-therapy practice, offering everything from food-sensitivity testing to yoga. And down on the ground floor, there's a wholefoods store that has won more awards than you can shake a stick at.

Specialities: McToucan burger, smoothies

The Shed
Smartie alecks

The result of an inspired redesign project on a grotty old toilet block, this sweet little café won over the locals as soon as it opened in 2013. But its success is not only down to its role in extinguishing one of the town's most notorious eyesores, but also the simplicity of its menu, the friendliness of its staff and the prettiness of its position in Goodland Gardens – a well-tended public space right on the River Tone.

The Shed offers gorgeous views and plenty of room for kids to run around – especially during the summer, when the outdoor seating area comes into its own. Reclaimed, mismatched furniture lends the interior a rustic charm.

Expect filling breakfast baps, typical lunchtime light bites, such as soup with crusty bread, enticing cakes and outstanding coffee.

Specialities: breakfast baps, coffee, Smartie shots

Mon–Sat 9–4   £

Goodland Gardens, The Bridge, Taunton TA1 1UQ, 01823 278 464

Getting There
By foot, head north over The Bridge and take the pedestrian exit on the right into Goodland Gardens. The Shed is nestled in among the flower beds next to the River Tone.

The Secret
Unexpected touches make this café stand out, from the blankets left outside on chilly days to the Smartie 'shots' served with every hot drink.

4
SERVICE

4
HEALTHY FOOD

4
AMBIENCE

72

Scarlett's Garden Café
A fabulous folly

5 SERVICE

5 HEALTHY FOOD

4 AMBIENCE

Apr–Nov Mon–Sat 10–4, Sun 11–3   ££

White Post Nursery, Langford Budville, Wellington TA21 0RW, 01823 401 517
www.scarlettsgarden.co.uk

Getting There
This café is found at the White Post Nursery in the village of Langford Budville, just outside Wellington.

The Secret
While you're here, stop by at White Post Nursery, which stocks all kinds of unusual plants that aren't generally available in larger garden centres.

Light floods in through the large French windows at Scarlett's Garden Café, a bijou wooden cabin in an idyllic rural setting. Although fairly compact, the cabin has a calm and comfortable atmosphere, even at busy times, thanks to its generously spaced tables.

The seasonal menu is simple but elegant. Expect everything from sourdough pizzas on Sundays to more sophisticated dishes, such as roasted beetroot with baked ricotta, fresh herbs, olives and griddled polenta. Puddings usually feature fruit, in some shape or form.

Scarlett's is also known for its fantastic afternoon teas, which vary from month to month. A typical summer option might be gravadlax bruschetta with lemon and dill ricotta and salad followed by two warm scones with loganberry jam and clotted cream.

Specialities: pizzas, puddings, afternoon tea

Silvers Pantry
The brunch bunch

SERVICE
5

HEALTHY FOOD
4

AMBIENCE
4

Tue–Sat 9–4.30 £

Prockters Farm, West Monkton,
Taunton TA2 8QN, 01823 413 443
www.willowsofsomerset.co.uk

Getting There
Head north out of Taunton on the
A3259, through Monkton Heathfield
and then left onto Blundells Lane.
Silvers Pantry is well signposted.

The Secret
*Chef and co-owner Stephen trained in
some of the finest establishments in
London, including restaurants owned
by Jamie Oliver and Gordon Ramsay.*

At Silvers Pantry, brunch lasts all day. Typical dishes include eggs Benedict – made using local asparagus, Parma ham and homemade hollandaise sauce – smoked salmon with scrambled eggs and buttermilk pancakes. Porridge fans can enjoy their daily fix with such indulgent toppings as berries and dark muscovado sugar.

Also on offer are doorstop sandwiches, pies and daily lunch specials, such as heirloom tomato salad with buffalo mozzarella, Parmesan, pesto, chilli, balsamic vinegar and pumpkin seeds. Afterwards, team up a slice of delicious cake with a mug of Silvers Pantry own-blend coffee, or skip all that and go for one of the sizable afternoon teas.

The small delicatessen attached to the café is a great place to buy unusual and exotic treats.

Specialities: polenta cake, eggs Benedict, coffee

The Crafty Teacup Café
Bunting & baking

The interior of The Crafty Teacup Café is a colourful mishmash of handmade bunting, paper flowers and mobiles. Most of the decoration has been made in the craft studio above, which offers workshops, classes and other arty parties, from hen dos to baby showers.

Seasonal, traditional fare is the order of the day in the café, with soups, ploughman's lunches, jacket potatoes, paninis, sandwiches and salads filling the pages of the large and varied menu. Try the mouthwatering grilled halloumi and roasted vegetables brushed with garlic. The high tea and cakes are also lovely.

Everything in the café is handmade to order, as it is in the craft studio above. Before you arrive, take a look at the website for details of classes available, and plan a day of eating and art.

Specialities: ploughman's lunches, high tea, cakes

Mon–Sat 10–4   ££

57B Victoria Street, Burnham-on-Sea
TA8 1AW, 01278 793 493
www.thecraftyteacup.co.uk

Getting There
From the Esplanade on the seafront, head up Vicarage Street and then turn left onto Victoria Street. The Crafty Teacup is on the corner on your right.

The Secret
If you visit on a Saturday morning and want to enjoy a child-free cake and coffee session, send your kids upstairs to the Crafty Kids' Club.

SERVICE

HEALTHY FOOD

AMBIENCE

PJ's Ice Cream Parlour
Fifty shades of ice

5 SERVICE

3 HEALTHY FOOD

4 AMBIENCE

Daily 10.30–6 (check ahead for winter hours)

£

2 Royal Parade, Weston-super-Mare BS23 1AJ, 07982 259 749

Getting There
Head for the seafront and the Grand Pier in Weston-super-Mare. PJ's is opposite the entrance to the pier.

The Secret
PJ's has a knack for coming up with zany concoctions for kids, such as the bubblegum-flavoured knickerbocker glory with hundreds and thousands and extra cream. Brace yourself for the sugar high!

Don't be put off by the garish picture menus at PJ's Ice Cream Parlour. This friendly seafront outfit offers a jaw-dropping 50-plus flavours, from Jaffa Cake to coconut to blackcurrant and clotted cream (made with real blackcurrants). They come in all shapes and sizes, including scoops, cones, coke floats, milkshakes and sundaes.

Those with special dietary requirements will be relieved to know there are also plenty of gluten-free ice creams and cones on offer here, as well as dairy-free ice creams and milkshakes.

Don't forget your bucket and spade when you visit PJ's – it's virtually on the beach, so there's no excuse not to burn off your icy indulgence with some paddling and sandcastle-building.

Specialities: all 50 flavours, dairy-free sundaes

The Blitz Tearoom
Tea at the Blitz

Tea at The Blitz is an experience of vintage glamour, with waitresses dressed up as 1940s' sweethearts, their lipstick and curls complementing the wartime artefacts that grace the walls. As you leaf through the ration book-style menu, listening to songs from the period blaring out from the gramophone, you'd be forgiven for thinking you'd travelled back in time.

Unsurprisingly, the menu is inspired by traditional British home cooking, particularly wartime recipes. Enjoy a full English breakfast with a nostalgia-inducing treat, such as Camp Coffee, Bovril, Ovaltine or even Victorian lemonade. Or there's the old-fashioned high tea, which features delicious cakes, scones and sandwiches (corned-beef or Spam, anyone?) presented on an elegant tiered stand – a very stylish way to enjoy afternoon tea.

Specialities: full English, toasties, Victorian lemonade

Mon–Fri 10–5, Sat 9–6, Sun 10–4

£

22 Waterloo Street, Weston-super-Mare BS23 1LN, 07854 089 121
www.facebook.com/theblitztearoom1940

Getting There
From the pier, go north along the Royal Parade and turn right onto Knightstone Road, which becomes Waterloo Street. The tearoom is on your right.

The Secret
This tearoom holds private parties and themed nights during which singers modelling themselves on Vera Lynn evoke the spirit of the age.

4
SERVICE

3
HEALTHY FOOD

4
AMBIENCE

RAILWAY CARRIAGE CAFE

The Trading Post
All aboard!

5 SERVICE

5 HEALTHY FOOD

4 AMBIENCE

Mon–Sat 9–5 **£**

The Old Filling Station, Lopenhead
TA13 5JH, 01460 241 666
www.tradingpostorganics.co.uk

Getting There
Head south from Ilchester on the
A303 and come off at the roundabout
signposted towards Lopen. The café
is 2km down the road, on the left.

The Secret
*This carriage was one of 3,000 built
in the late 19th century for use on the
Great Eastern Lines out of London's
Liverpool Street Station.*

This quirky café occupies a beautifully restored railway
carriage from the 1880s. With its shared tables,
reclaimed benches and old leather sofas, there's
room for about 22 'passengers'. Like most railway
carriages, there's a constant stream of people coming
and going – only, in the case of the Trading Post, it
has nothing to do with commuting convenience and
everything to do with lovely food and surroundings.

Adjacent to a brilliantly stocked farm shop, this café
boasts a daily-changing menu based on what comes
in fresh from the fields. Sample the wholesome
butternut squash, beetroot and feta-cheese tart or
minted-pea soup. There's also a collection of tasty
homemade desserts, as well as takeaway bites from
the farm shop. Although there is wheelchair access to
the shop, there's none to the café.

Specialities: soup, salads, tarts, cakes

Gooey chocolate brownie

Early Doors
Born in a barn

4
SERVICE

3
HEALTHY
FOOD

4
AMBIENCE

Daily midday–10 (check website for special events)   **£**

Latches Lane Crossroads,
Draycott Road, Cheddar
BS27 3YB, 07789 790 427
www.earlydoorsbarn.com

Getting There
This cider and ale barn is situated on the northwest side of Draycott, on Draycott Road (A371).

The Secret
There's a 45-minute walking route to Early Doors from Cheddar village – no designated driver required!

For a long time a redundant farm workshop, this giant shed has been converted into a cider and ale barn that couldn't be further from your run-of-the-mill drinking venue. The décor is something of a hotchpotch, and yet it's homely, with sofas, standard lamps and rugs. There's even a sunny back yard, which has great views.

Early Doors is at the heart of rural Somerset's drinking scene – both literally and metaphorically. Stop in for a pint of local ale or cider with some melt-in-the-mouth pork-pie slices, a casserole or a platter of 'Somerset tapas', which comes with pickled eggs, pickled onions and snacky cheese offerings. The menu description of the BLT – it includes smoky bacon, Draycott blue and 'other stuff' – speaks volumes about the down-to-earth character of this cavernous gathering place.

Specialities: chilli jam on Ritz Crackers, veggie chilli

Goodfellows
Continental drift

Goodfellows, located slap-bang in the middle of medieval Wells, is a magnet for fans of fine dining. Expect light and delicate seafood dishes enhanced with beautifully flavoured oils, vinegars and dressings. Though dishes here have a distinctly Continental accent – chef and co-owner Adam Fellows has worked in kitchens across France and Belgium – ingredients are almost all local. The fish and shellfish, for example, come from the small seaside town of Brixham in Devon.

The restaurant has three dining rooms, the most popular of which is an open-plan space where you can watch the chefs hard at work in the kitchen. Alternatively, there's a dining room at the front, which overlooks Sadler Street, or a more intimate space in the eaves. Look out for the mural caricatures of the owners and chefs, created by a local artist.

Specialities: seafood, patisserie, five-course tasting menu

Mon–Sat 9/10–4, also Wed & Thu/Fri & Sat 6–9.30/10   ££

5 Sadler Street, Wells BA5 2RR
01749 673 866
www.goodfellowswells.co.uk

Getting There
Goodfellows is on Sadler Street in central Wells, directly opposite the HSBC bank.

The Secret
The patisserie next door, which has the same owners as the restaurant, uses French and local flours in its fresh bread. Drop in for éclairs, tarts, truffles, pastries or a light lunch.

5
SERVICE

4
HEALTHY FOOD

4
AMBIENCE

Homemade chocolates, Goodfellows

Square Edge Café
Come into the parlour

4

SERVICE

4

HEALTHY FOOD

4

AMBIENCE

Tue–Sat 9–5.30   ££

2 Town Hall Buildings, Market Place,
Wells BA5 1SE, 01749 671 166
www.facebook.com/squareedgecafe

Getting There
Square Edge Café can be found in
the Town Hall Buildings, on the edge
of the cobbled Market Square in the
centre of Wells.

The Secret
*You can try dishes from far-flung
places at the exciting global-food
events held at Square Edge Café. Call
for details and always book ahead.*

Square Edge Café occupies an 18th-century building
that's said to be home to a friendly ghost. At one time
a prison refectory, the space was, until recently, the
café owner's front room. Pick a table in the parlour or
dining room and take a moment to appreciate the funky
vintage and kitsch artefacts that cover the walls.

The menu includes everything from breakfast dishes,
such as bacon butties and American-style pancakes
with maple syrup, to a great range of wraps, baps,
soups and salads. There are also daily specials, roasts
on Sundays and a splendid selection of home-baked
cakes to sink your teeth into.

At the back of the café, you'll find a sweet courtyard
and covered area with beautifully mismatched seating,
vintage sheet-metal posters and exposed brickwork.

Specialities: seafood risotto, prawn and chorizo salad

Hartley's Kitchen
Breakfast bonanza

4

SERVICE

4

HEALTHY
FOOD

4

AMBIENCE

Tue–Sat 8–4, Sun 9–2.30   **££**

Rookery Farm, Binegar
BA3 4UL, 01749 841 718
www.hartleyskitchen.com

Getting There

From Shepton Mallet, head north
on the A37 towards Bristol. Turn
left onto the B3135, and Rookery
Farm is on your right-hand side.

The Secret

*If you appreciate antiques, follow your
meal with a visit to the vintage clock
shop or the auction house, also on the
farm. Check auction dates online.*

The breakfast menu at Hartley's Kitchen is enough
to get anyone's taste buds going. It mixes up all the
usual suspects – a full English and eggs Benedict,
Florentine and Royale, for example – with a range of
imaginative extras, such as a smoked-salmon bagel,
croque monsieur and smoked kippers. There are also
American-style pancakes with crispy bacon, porridge
topped with raspberries, Greek yoghurt and honey,
and croissants dusted with dark chocolate. Breakfast
is served all day throughout the week, but finishes at
11.30am on Sundays to give the kitchen time to prepare
its wildly popular roast lunch.

The décor here may be jaded, but the jolly staff, vibrant
feel and satisfying food more than make up for that. It's
worth booking in advance, as it gets busy at peak times.

Specialities: American-style pancakes, full English
breakfast, Sunday lunches

Bean Shot Coffee
Roasting the right way

While there's no escaping the fact that you're sitting in an industrial unit at Bean Shot Coffee, it doesn't diminish the unforgettable experience of sipping an intensely aromatic brew while watching the master roasters at work behind the viewing window.

The art of coffee making is at the forefront of everything that happens at Bean Shot Coffee, from sourcing the best beans to roasting and brewing them to exacting standards. This is the place to visit if you want to sample outstanding coffee, grab a bag of great-quality beans or pick up some insider information on how to make the perfect brew at home.

Just join one of the popular tasting events, and you'll be guided through the entire coffee-making process, from bean to brew.

Speciality: quite simply, coffee!

Mon–Sat 8.30–5 £

The Roastery, The Old Mill, Station Road, Bruton BA10 0EH, 01749 813 180
www.beanshot.co.uk

Getting There
Take the B3081 out of Bruton towards Charlton Musgrove and you'll see signs for Bean Shot Coffee at the Old Mill Business Park on the edge of town.

The Secret
In 2015, Bean Shot Coffee won the Best Coffee Roasted in the UK award in the UK Coffee Stop Awards; votes were cast by 60,000 British coffee-lovers.

4
SERVICE

3
HEALTHY FOOD

3
AMBIENCE

At the Chapel
Bread & wine

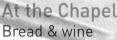

5 SERVICE

5 HEALTHY FOOD

4 AMBIENCE

Mon–Sat 7–9.30,
Sun midday–8

££

High Street, Bruton BA10 0AE
01749 814 070
www.atthechapel.co.uk

Getting There
At the Chapel is easily located on
Bruton High Street (A359); look
out for the historic chapel façade.
There's plenty of street parking.

The Secret
*Regular events are held in the smart
and informal clubroom here, including
live-music nights, talks with writers,
pop-up shops and yoga sessions.*

Set in a beautifully converted, Grade II-listed chapel,
this restaurant is a spectacular place to eat. Light
streams in from the towering chapel windows, setting
the bright white interior aglow, while tall church
candles on elegant wrought-iron stands are lit at night,
adding to the sense of heritage and harmony.

The eclectic menu features West Country produce,
such as watercress risotto with Dorset Blue Vinney
and Cornish hake with brown shrimp butter. Offbeat
wines, mainly from small producers, make the perfect
accompaniment to all these local flavours.

The on-site bakery contains a vast wood-fired oven.
From here, Venetian-trained chefs turn out fresh
loaves and simple but superb pizzas every day of the
week, as well as afternoon teas throughout the day.

Specialities: bakery goods, pizzas, wines

Café at the Grain
Music & muffins

4

SERVICE

4

HEALTHY FOOD

4

AMBIENCE

Mon–Sat 9–5, Sun 10–1   £

Cheese and Grain, Market Yard,
Frome BA11 1BE, 01373 455 420
www.cheeseandgrain.com/cafe

Getting There
Follow the A36 and the B3090 into
town and park in the car park beside
the Black Swan Arts Centre. The
Cheese and Grain is at the far end.

The Secret
The secret of this venue is its versatility:
follow lunch with a live-music show, a
car-boot sale or even – if you pick the
right day – the annual tattoo convention.

The Cheese & Grain in Frome is a member-owned
social enterprise and charity located in an old market
hall. Café, bar and live-music venue rolled into one,
the initiative was launched to support and promote the
social, cultural and economic life of the local area.

The friendly on-site café, which has plenty of outdoor
seating and a popular play area, has built up a great
reputation for its food and drink. Expect interesting
salads and an array of savoury snacks, as well as cakes
and bakes. The nectarine and raspberry upside-down
cake goes well with a cup of the café's expertly made
coffee. For lunch, try the basil, olive, pepper and cheese
muffins or a slice of homemade quiche.

Work from the Cheese & Grain's Artist of the Month is
on display in the café and foyer.

Specialities: cakes, quiches, savoury muffins

NECTARINE AND RASPBERRY GLUTEN + DAIRY FREE £2.50

Delis,
Bakeries &
Suppliers

Southwest England
Delis, Bakeries & Suppliers

VENUES

		page
86	Da Bara Bakery	152
87	The Cornish Maids Fudge Shop	154
88	Sarah's Pasty Shop	155
89	Country Cheeses	156
90	Blacks Delicatessen	157
91	The Fish Deli	158
92	Dartmoor Butchers	160
93	Mulberry Manor	161
94	Olives Et Al	162
95	The Salt Pig	164
96	The Bakery	166
97	The Mall Deli	167
98	The Fine Cheese Co.	168
99	The Bertinet Bakery	170
100	Brown and Forrest	171
101	Pumpkin Delicatessen and Café	172
102	Queen Street Delicatessen	174
103	The Good Earth	176

Da Bara Bakery
Good bread

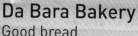 

4
SERVICE

3
HEALTHY FOOD

3
AMBIENCE

Mon–Fri 7–3,
Sat & Sun 7–12.30

£

Unit 1D, Grampound Road Industrial Estate, Truro, Cornwall TR2 4TB
01726 882 096
www.dabara.co.uk

Getting There
From the A390, head north towards Grampound Road. The industrial estate is on the left.

The Secret
A love of French bread inspired the owners to open Da Bara, where French recipes are used and a French wood carving is on display. Vive la France!

An industrial estate might not be the most appealing location for a bakery, but the brothers who own Da Bara – which means 'good bread' in Cornish – have made it work by relying on the expertise of their millers and bakers to draw custom. The sourdough loaves and baguettes are prime examples of this skill, their slightly charred, crunchy crusts giving way to perfectly soft centres. Tea breads, pastries and brownies – to eat in or take away – are from tried-and-tested recipes, baked on the premises and best enjoyed with a fair-trade coffee.

A perk of the bakery's industrial-estate location is that the team has room to bake enough delectable dough to be able to supply other businesses, while retaining that distinctive homemade quality. So if you can't get here, look out for Da Bara products in local shops, hotels and restaurants, including Jamie Oliver's Fifteen Cornwall.

Specialities: sourdough, granola, cinnamon buns

Ciabatta
72.00

The Cornish Maids Fudge Shop
Funky fudge

5 SERVICE

2 HEALTHY FOOD

4 AMBIENCE

Summer 10–5, winter 11–4

£

The Coombes, Polperro, Cornwall PL13 2RQ, 01503 272 001

Getting There
Polperro's car park is easily found as you approach the village. From here, walk down into the village and the shop is the first you come to; it's on the right-hand side of the road, opposite the doctors' surgery.

The Secret
In our opinion, this is the best fudge recipe in Cornwall – a family secret for more than 50 years.

The original clotted-cream fudge recipe, which has been passed down through the generations, has made Cornish Maids a Mecca for sweet teeth and happily helped a few dentists to early retirement. Alongside this melt-in-the-mouth deliciousness, it sells a whole host of other exotic and unusual fudge flavours. Try the chocolate chilli or cappuccino – and buy them by the bar, bag or box.

But the delicacies don't stop at fudge. Fluffy marshmallow, chocolates, jams, pickles and chutneys can all be bought and wrapped up as gifts. There are ready-made hampers for sale or you can bundle your favourites into a big bespoke box of wicker wickedness. You can even ask for your goodies to be shipped halfway around the world. Cornish Maids is rotting teeth waiting to happen, but that's why we love it.

Specialities: bespoke gift hampers, fudge flavours, homemade marshmallow

Sarah's Pasty Shop
Pick of the pasties

Many Cornish pasty shops are worthy of a recommendation, but the exceptional pasties at Sarah's make it the only one featured in this book. As you'd expect, thin, crisp and flaky pastry encases generous fillings to create plump and appealing pasties. The traditional recipe of minced beef, swede and black pepper is brilliantly recreated here, and is the firm favourite of locals who know and love the establishment. Other fillings compete with gusto for their attention, though, such as the mackerel and horseradish – surprisingly good, even though it might sound all wrong.

With interesting ideas and specials, such as Fishy Friday and Pie of the Month, to keep the menu fresh, this place has cornered the Cornish takeaway market in Polperro. Once you've grabbed your freshly cooked bundle, head down to the seafront to enjoy it.

Specialities: traditional pasties with imaginative fillings, Pie of the Month

Mon–Sat 9–4, Sun 10–4   £

6 Buller Street, East Looe, Cornwall
PL13 1AS, 01503 263 973
www.sarahspastyshop.com

Getting There
Wander down through Looe until you get to Buller Street. Sarah's Pasty Shop is a few doors down on the right-hand side.

The Secret
This tiny bakery, which has been open for 26 years, occupies the old net stores at the bottom of a traditional fishing cottage near the harbour in Looe.

4
SERVICE

3
HEALTHY FOOD

3
AMBIENCE

Country Cheeses
The crème de la crème

5 SERVICE

3 HEALTHY FOOD

3 AMBIENCE

Mon–Sat 9.30–5   ££

Market Road, Tavistock, Devon
PL19 0BW, 01822 615 035
www.countrycheeses.co.uk

Getting There
Country Cheeses is on Market Road,
which is the lane behind the Pannier
Market right in the heart of Tavistock.

The Secret
*Owners Gary and Elise also run the
town's Real Cheese Fair, where
local producers discuss the animal
husbandry, ingredients, science and
art that go into every delicious roundel.*

Twenty-five years ago, this remarkable little shop
started as a stall in Tavistock's Pannier Market, selling
just six different West Country cheeses. Today, there
are three shops – including branches in Totnes and
Topsham – bringing together a variety of cheeses from
the best artisan producers across the southwest.

On a hot summer's day, your nose will lead you
straight to the front door of this shop. Inside, you'll be
invited to sample as many different varieties as you like,
from butter-soft, creamy goat's cheeses and strong
cheddars to the crumbliest, bluest Stiltons.

Prepare to be impressed – as the Conservative politician
and former editor of *The Ecologist*, Zac Goldsmith, says,
the 100-plus handmade cheeses sold here give most
French cheeses a serious run for their money.

Specialities: blue vinney, Keen's extra-mature cheddar

Blacks Delicatessen
A moorland retreat

If you're heading out onto the moors, Blacks is a great place to stock up on supplies. The homemade quiches, fresh bread, local cheddar and spicy salami in this Devon deli make the most superb picnic lunches. Throw in a sweet treat and a coffee to go, and you'll be set.

If you're eating in, the open-air tables are the place to be – sit out at the front, amid the activity of the town, or around the back, where the tranquillity of the nearby churchyard is mesmerising. Those visiting in chillier times can enjoy a cup of piping-hot soup on one of the sought-after window stools and watch the world go by.

If you want to share the magic of Blacks with someone else – or simply want to prolong your own experience – pick up a pre-made hamper or put together a bespoke one yourself.

Specialities: quiches, pies, coffee

Mon–Sat 9–5.30   ££

28 The Square, Chagford, Devon
TQ13 8AB, 01647 433 545
www.blacks-deli.com

Getting There
This deli is located slap-bang in the middle of the old stannary town of Chagford, with parking nearby.

The Secret
Blacks redefines the concept of ready meals, with exquisite soups made fresh every day and hearty homemade dishes featuring the highest-quality locally reared meat. Ready the freezer!

5
SERVICE

5
HEALTHY FOOD

4
AMBIENCE

The Fish Deli
Packed to the gills with fish

5
SERVICE

5
HEALTHY FOOD

4
AMBIENCE

Mon–Sat 9–5   ££

7 East Street, Ashburton, Devon
TQ13 7AD, 01364 654 833
www.thefishdeli.co.uk

Getting There
The Fish Deli is on the main road in Ashburton, opposite St Lawrence Lane. There is plenty of street parking nearby.

The Secret
If it's summer and you're in barbecue mode, you can pick up a selection of freshly prepared fish kebabs, fish burgers and stuffed and wrapped extras here – time to get sizzling!

The Fish Deli in Ashburton is a wonderland for anyone who loves preparing, cooking and eating fresh seafood. Sustainable fishing is the running theme here, with the bright-eyed daily catches from boats in Looe and Plymouth filling the fabulous fresh-fish counter.

Homemade treats on offer include fresh fishcakes, curries, pies and pâtés. A giant tapas stand fills the centre of the shop, with bowls of stuffed red peppers, dark-green olives, sundried tomatoes, artichokes and other healthy morsels. There are also condiments, spices, cookbooks and fish-themed gifts for sale.

Along with the regular preparation advice you'd expect at a good fish counter, The Fish Deli offers recipe ideas when you buy something. The team is great at fielding questions, so don't be afraid to ask.

Speciality: fresh fish

Dartmoor Butchers
The meat of the matter

5
SERVICE

3
HEALTHY FOOD

2
AMBIENCE

Mon, Wed & Sat 7.30–1, Tue, Thu & Fri 7.30–4.30   £

28 East Street, Ashburton, Devon
TQ13 7AZ, 01364 654 600
www.dartmoorbutchers.co.uk

Getting There
East Street is the gentle hill climbing out of Ashburton town centre. Dartmoor Butchers can be found a little way up the hill on the right.

The Secret
The pie counter at this butcher sells all sorts of handmade pies, sausage rolls and 'Cornish' pasties – arguably the best you can find outside Cornwall.

Perched on the southern edge of Dartmoor, the former stannary town of Ashburton is the biggest community within the national park. The town is known for its impressive number of independent shops, including this busy butcher – a mainstay of the local area.

As you might expect, there's a constant supply of locally reared meat at Dartmoor Butchers, including beef, lamb, pork and poultry. Every cut you can imagine is available here, from rib and rump to topside and tongue. There's also a stock of home-cured bacon, cooked meats, black and hogs puddings, and even game – if you visit in the right season.

If you're planning a long walk on Dartmoor, stop off here first and fill your backpack with some fantastic-tasting fuel from the pie counter.

Specialities: local meat, pasties, sausage rolls

Mulberry Manor
Eyes on the pies

There doesn't appear to be anything out of the ordinary about Mulberry Manor when you approach it from the street. But when you sink your teeth into one of its golden pies, you'll easily believe the rumour that one of its most dedicated customers would regularly drive a 320km round trip to collect a freezer-load.

Traditional pork pies, sausage rolls, Scotch eggs, hand-crimped pasties and all sorts of veggie snacks fill the counter at this busy bakery, where original 17th-century features include beams, exposed stonework and an inglenook fireplace.

In summer, hordes of tourists gobble up their snacks on the cobbled curb outside. If you can hold on a moment longer, they taste even better on the beach.

Specialities: beef and Stilton pasty, cheese straws, pork pies

Mon–Sat 8.30–5   £

10 Broad Street, Lyme Regis, Dorset
DT7 3QD, 01297 444 613

Getting There
As you're walking down Broad Street towards the beach, Mulberry Manor is on the right-hand side, just as the shops become elevated from the road.

The Secret
Try the heart-shaped Gazillionaire at your peril – this infamous biscuit snack, which comes topped with generous layers of chocolate and caramel, is dangerously sweet.

5
SERVICE

3
HEALTHY FOOD

3
AMBIENCE

Olives Et Al
The world's your olive

5
SERVICE

5
HEALTHY FOOD

4
AMBIENCE

Mon–Sat 9–5.30   ££

1 North Dorset Business Park,
Rolls Mill Way, Sturminster Newton,
Dorset DT10 2GA, 01258 474 303
www.olivesetal.co.uk

Getting There
Olives Et Al is just off the A357, at
the entrance to the North Dorset
Business Park.

The Secret
*The oldest olive tree the team here has
encountered is in Crete – reputed to be
3,200 years old, this one-time Minoan
seedling still produces olives today.*

The chances are you'll have come across Olives Et Al
products before in the many shops and restaurants
it supplies. But there's nothing like enjoying them on
home turf, at this deli in Sturminster Newton.

From freshly baked breads, crackers and other savoury
nibbles to cheeses and delicious charcuterie, this
deli stocks just about everything you could need for a
delicious picnic, a tapas meal or a cocktail party. But
it's the olives that really steal the show – they come in
a variety of different marinades, from classic rosemary
and garlic to Moorish coriander and cumin. There are
even alcohol-steeped sorts for use in cocktails.

There are three other branches of Olives Et Al, in nearby
Poundbury, Cheddar in Somerset and Chichester in
West Sussex. It also has a well-stocked online deli.

Specialities: olives and other savoury snacks

SUNDRIED
TOMATO
STUFFED OLIVES

The Salt Pig
All-in-one shop

5 SERVICE

5 HEALTHY FOOD

4 AMBIENCE

Daily 8.30–7, also Thu–Sat 6–10

££

6 North Street, Wareham, Dorset BH20 4AF, 01929 550 673
www.thesaltpig.co.uk

Getting There
The Salt Pig is a couple of doors down from the NatWest bank on North Street (B3075) in Wareham.

The Secret
The Salt Pig's rare-breed woolly pigs perform an important function at the nearby nature reserve of RSPB Arne – their foraging habits are used to rejuvenate areas of tired heathland.

From the outside, The Salt Pig might look rather unassuming, but once you're inside, the exceptional produce is all that matters. Here, under one roof, you'll find a tiny fishmonger, butcher and deli. There's also a café-restaurant, which is open every day, as well as three nights a week, when the menu changes to à la carte.

All the meat on sale at The Salt Pig is reared within 12km of the shop and the charcuterie is made just 5km away. The freshly caught crabs and lobsters are landed at nearby Kimmeridge, while the fruit and vegetables are seasonal, local and very fresh. Members of staff are always on hand to talk you through the produce and its provenance.

If the café looks busy, don't despair – there's a room around the back with more seating.

Specialities: pork, charcuterie, apple and raisin pie

The Bakery
Let them eat cake

5 SERVICE

4 HEALTHY FOOD

4 AMBIENCE

Mon–Wed & Sat 8–4.30,
Thu 8–8, Fri 8–9

£

1 The Green, Sherborne,
Dorset DT9 3HY
01935 813 264

Getting There
Head up the hill through the town
of Sherborne and The Bakery is at
the junction of Higher Cheap Street
and The Green.

The Secret
*The Bakery's 'pizza bread' is superb.
With a combination of herby pizza
dough, olive oil, red pepper and onion,
it's like a savoury Chelsea bun!*

The comforting aroma of freshly baked goods spills out
of The Bakery every time someone opens the front door,
coaxing you in from the street. Downstairs, you'll find
a traditional bakery offering all sorts of doughy goods,
while upstairs is a characterful little café in the loft
where you can sit down and enjoy them.

Running down the middle of the café is a communal
trestle table lined with bowls of thick butter curls and
jugs of water. Sit on the long bench, made from great
chunks of wood and topped with tractor seats, and take
your time over a bowl of soup, a Dorset rarebit or slice
of scrumptious apple and cinnamon polenta cake.

At weekends, The Bakery opens late for a £10-a-head
sourdough pizza feast known for its selection of
toppings and BYO policy.

Specialities: sourdough pizzas, apple and polenta cake

Chorizo Sausage Roll
Free range sausage meat, chorizo chunks & chilli flakes.
£2.00 take-away
£2.40 in the cafe
Made by us...

Ploughman's Sausage Roll
Free-range sausage meat, mature Cheddar & onion marmalade.
£2.00 take-away
£2.40 in the cafe
Made by us...

Black Pudding Sausage Roll

The Mall Deli
Scotch-egg city

The counter and shelves at this deli groan under the weight of all the dried and preserved goods for which it's become known. Expect everything from pies and pâtés to cheeses and cured meats – oh, and an astonishing 40-plus varieties of Scotch egg.

At the back of the shop is a pretty café, where you can enjoy a coffee and slice of cake or something more substantial – the Mall Deli Plate and the charcuterie selection are both really good. While you're waiting for your food, take a look at the local artworks on display.

Only a short stroll from gorgeous Bristol Down, this deli is a great place to buy picnic ingredients. For a lovely light lunch, go for fresh bread, honey-roast ham, Barkham blue cheese and crisp white wine. And a Scotch egg, of course – it would be rude not to.

Specialities: Mall Deli Plate, Scotch eggs, cupcakes

Mon–Fri 9.30–5, Sat 9–6, Sun 11–5   ££

14 The Mall, Clifton, Bristol
BS8 4DR, 0117 973 4440
www.themalldeli.co.uk

Getting There
You'll find The Mall Deli among the charming shops and cafés of Clifton Village. Just 2 minutes' walk north lies gorgeous Clifton Down.

The Secret
If you give a few days' notice, you can order pretty much any cake you like, from sparkly cupcakes to customised gluten- and dairy-free creations.

5
SERVICE

5
HEALTHY FOOD

4
AMBIENCE

The Fine Cheese Co.
Cheese please

5

SERVICE

3

HEALTHY
FOOD

3

AMBIENCE

Mon–Sat 8–5 (café),
9–5 (shop)

££

29 & 31 Walcot Street, Bath
BA1 5BN, 01225 483 407
www.finecheese.co.uk

Getting There
The Fine Cheese Co. is easily found on
Walcot Street, close to the River Avon
and opposite the Hilton Hotel. There
are plenty of car parks nearby.

The Secret
*This shop offers luxury gift items
to suit everyone from cheese
connoisseurs and booze-lovers to
sugar addicts and young palates.*

You can tell how seriously the business of cheese is
taken here by the sheer variety on display and the
energy and expertise of the staff, who are more than
happy to help if you're feeling flummoxed.

Whether you're after soft, hard, blue, goat's, mature,
mild or stinky, you're guaranteed to find what you want
on the jam-packed shelves of The Fine Cheese Co. Pick
up something to go with it, such as a loaf of fresh bread,
crackers, olives, chutneys, pickles, charcuterie and
antipasti items, or even a bottle of fine port. Afterwards,
swing by the café next door, which is part of the same
business, for a cheese platter or Welsh rarebit.

And if you want to feed your cheese habit when you're
back at home, visit the online shop, voted the best
supplier of mail-order cheese by *The Telegraph*.

Specialities: cheeses, chocolates, wines

The Bertinet Bakery
Bready bliss

5
SERVICE

4
HEALTHY FOOD

4
AMBIENCE

Mon–Sat 8–6 £

1 New Bond Street Place, Bath
BA1 1BH, 01225 445 531
www.bertinet.com

Getting There
New Bond Street Place is the little
pedestrianised shopping lane that
links Upper Borough Walls and
New Bond Street.

The Secret
*Award-winning international chef,
author and teacher Richard Bertinet
bakes the diverse artisan breads and
pastries sold here.*

The Bertinet Bakery is the most authentic artisan
bakery in Bath. The enticing smell of baking bread will
hit you long before you see the front door, and, once
inside, you'll be amazed by the sheer diversity of items
on offer. Sourdough, spelt, ciabatta and rye loaves fill
the shelves alongside specials such as rosemary and
rock-salt focaccia and Provençal olive and lavender loaf.

But that's not all. Nearby, at 12 St Andrew's Terrace,
is the Bertinet Kitchen – a cookery school with an
excellent reputation. Here, you can learn the art of
baking and bread-making, or attend master classes
in Indian, Asian, French, Italian and traditional British
cuisine. There are also courses for people on restricted
diets and for those who are daunted by cooking fish
and seafood. So, if you like cooking as well as eating,
Bertinet's offers the best of both worlds.

Specialities: sourdough, salted-caramel buns

Brown and Forrest
Blowing hot and cold

Family-run Brown and Forrest smokery is bursting at the seams with all kinds of traditional wood-fired, hot-smoked foods, such as eel, salmon and trout. More unusual products include cold-smoked cheddar and garlic bulbs, and whole fillets of smoked lamb.

Next to the shop is an award-winning restaurant where you can sample these flavoursome goods, often straight from the smokery. The menu also features homemade soup, cakes and desserts, including Brown and Forrest's trademark bread and butter pudding.

If you'd like a behind-the-scenes look at this fascinating place, sign up for one of the tours to meet the experts and see how the hot- and cold-smoking processes work. If your wallet allows, leave with one of the hefty hampers.

Specialities: smoked eel, duck and salmon, bread and butter pudding

Mon–Sat 9–4   ££

Bowdens Farm Smokery, Hambridge, Somerset TA10 0BP
01458 250 875
www.smokedeel.co.uk

Getting There
From the village of Curry Rivel, take the B3168 towards Hambridge and Westport, and keep an eye out for the sign to Brown and Forrest on your left.

The Secret
This smokery supplies Fortnum & Mason, as well as restaurants owned by chefs Tom Kerridge and Rick Stein.

5 SERVICE

4 HEALTHY FOOD

4 AMBIENCE

Pumpkin Delicatessen and Café
Home comforts

SERVICE 5

HEALTHY FOOD 5

AMBIENCE 5

Mon–Sat 8.30–5   ££

1 The Borough Mall, Wedmore,
Somerset BS28 4EB
01934 713 289
www.pumpkinwedmore.co.uk

Getting There
Pumpkin is easily found in the heart
of Wedmore, next to the post office.

The Secret
*Beautiful food items prepared by
this deli-café have appeared on the
cover of regional lifestyle magazine
Somerset Life as a showcase of
the perfect picnic.*

The drive through the picturesque Somerset Levels
to the idyllic village of Wedmore is half the fun of a visit
to Pumpkin Delicatessen and Café, where you can sit
in a pretty, flower-filled garden or the homely interior,
depending on the season.

The small but well-stocked deli counter here features
dozens of different sweet and savoury treats. Kick off
the day with a freshly baked croissant and creamy hot
chocolate, or dive straight into lunch, with its salads,
sandwiches, pies, homemade soups and quiches, which
are packed with fresh, seasonal ingredients. And if you
get there later in the day, pair a slice of homemade cake
(the brownies are famous) with a cup of tea or coffee.

Before you head home, check out the selection of
pantry essentials on sale at the deli counter.

Specialities: homemade cakes, broccoli and Stilton soup

Queen Street Delicatessen
Great for grazing

5
SERVICE

5
HEALTHY FOOD

4
AMBIENCE

Mon–Sat 9–5   ££

14 Queen Street, Wells, Somerset
BA5 2DP, 01749 679 803
www.queenstreetdeli.co.uk

Getting There
This deli is in the city centre. There's
street parking outside, although it's
worth finding a car park and staying
on longer so you can explore.

The Secret
*Although there's no café here, coffee
and – in the colder months – freshly
made hot soup are served to take
away with sandwiches and baguettes.*

Wells is a great destination for those who love good
food, and this classic delicatessen is firmly on the
need-to-know map in England's smallest medieval city.

You'll find everything you'd expect from a top-quality
deli here, including outstanding imported olive oils,
freshly baked loaves and seeded baps, as well as hams,
olives, local cheeses and handmade ice creams. You
can also order beef to be delivered here from Brown
Cow Organics – a brand that's favoured by chefs Hugh
Fearnley-Whittingstall, Rick Stein and Jamie Oliver.

Queen Street Delicatessen is the ideal place to grab
gourmet goodies for a picnic lunch. Just five minutes'
walk away lie the grounds of Wells Cathedral – the
perfect place for a lazy afternoon's grazing.

Specialities: pies and quiches, breads, local cheeses,
ice creams

SOMERSET CHEESE COMPANY

Six Spires

Hard Cheese made from Unpasteurised
Cow's milk

DITCHEAT HILL FARM · DITCHEAT · SOMERSET · BA4 6TL

The Good Earth
Forty years of good food

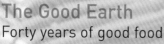 

5

SERVICE

5

HEALTHY FOOD

5

AMBIENCE

Mon–Fri 9–4.30, Sat 9–5   ££

4–6 Priory Road, Wells, Somerset
BA5 1SY, 01749 678 600
www.thegoodearthwells.co.uk

Getting There
From Wells High Street, head south
onto Broad Street and continue on it
until it becomes Priory Road. You'll
find The Good Earth on your right.

The Secret
The Good Earth began life as a self-
sufficiency store back in the 1970s
– a philosophy it champions to this
day, in its local, seasonal ingredients.

Scrubbed-pine tables, church pews, window shutters,
wooden floors and rustic candle-holders lend The Good
Earth its appealing country-kitchen interior – a warm
and welcoming place where the idea of tucking into a
homemade dish made with local, seasonal produce
comes very naturally indeed.

Expect a couple of hot main courses each day, such as
vegetable lasagne and root-vegetable cottage pie, as
well as a range of light-lunch choices, from salads and
soups to quiches and jacket potatoes.

While you're here, take time to notice the limited-
edition prints and original works by local artists
hanging on the walls, check out the homeware, gifts
and curiosities in the classy shop and stock up on larder
essentials in the wholefoods store.

Specialities: seasonal dishes, vegan food

Carrot and Walnut Cake

Farms,
Markets &
Street Food

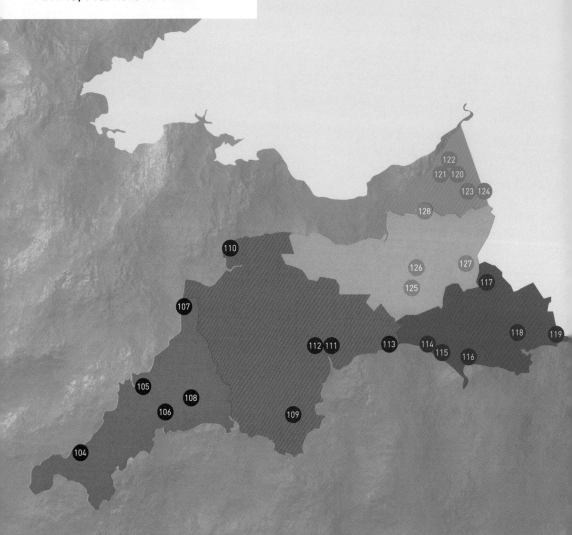

Southwest England
Farms, Markets & Street Food

VENUES

		page
104	Trevaskis Farm Shop	182
105	St Kew Harvest Farm Shop	184
106	Kernow Forno	186
107	Rectory Farm Tea Rooms	187
108	Inkie's Smokehouse BBQ	188
109	Riverford	189
110	Seadog	190
111	Darts Farm	192
112	Oasis Falafel and Grill	194
113	Felicity's Farm Shop	195
114	Downhouse Farm Garden Café	196
115	Rachel's	198
116	Eweleaze Farm	200
117	The Udder Farm Shop	202
118	Barford Ice Cream Garden	204
119	The Steak Out	205
120	The Bristol Sausage Shop	206
121	Eat a Pitta	207
122	The Better Food Company	208
123	Bath Farmers' Market	210
124	Funghi Fruits	211
125	Somerset Cider Brandy Company	212
126	Pitney Farm Shop	214
127	Kimbers' Farm Shop	215
128	Lye Cross Farm Shop	216

Trevaskis Farm Shop
Down on the farm

4 SERVICE

5 HEALTHY FOOD

4 AMBIENCE

Daily 8–8 ££

Connor Downs, Hayle, Cornwall
R27 5JQ, 01209 713 931
www.trevaskisfarm.co.uk

Getting There
On the road linking Camborne and
Hayle, turn south onto Gwinear Road
at Connor Downs. The farm is very
well signposted.

The Secret
*Trevaskis sells rare-breed British Lop
pork, which has been bred here since
1863. The excellent quality of the meat
is evident in its flavour and succulence.*

Trevaskis Farm Shop showcases high-quality, locally
produced goods, from fresh fruit and vegetables to
baked goods, eggs, cheese, fish, meat and wine.

The butcher's counter stocks all the usual suspects, as
well as seasonal varieties, such as venison, pheasant
and wild boar. The contents of the fish counter varies
from day to day, depending on what's been landed that
morning in nearby Newlyn, and the cheese counter
stocks various Cornish varieties, including Helford
White, St Endellion Brie and Cornish Blue, as well as
popular cheeses from around the world.

The huge on-site restaurant is open from 8.30 every
day. While you're here, enjoy the pick-your-own
orchards, kitchen gardens and animal enclosures.
Entrance is free, making it a perfect family outing.

Specialities: British Lop pork, sausages, bread, cakes

St Kew Harvest Farm Shop
Join the club

3

SERVICE

3

HEALTHY FOOD

3

AMBIENCE

Tue–Fri 10–5, also Tue–Sat 7–10 (closed Jan Fri nights) **£**

St Kew Highway, Bodmin, Cornwall PL30 3EF, 01208 841 818
www.facebook.com/stkewharvest

Getting There
Heading northeast on the A39 out of Wadebridge, you'll see the farm shop on the left-hand side, next to St Kew Golf Course.

The Secret
As a member of St Kew's Cornish Bread Club, you receive a knock-down rate on the accredited Bread Master Class at River Cottage Chefs' School.

A farm shop with a difference, St Kew's sells bread and pizzas straight from an on-site wood-fired oven, as well as all the usual suspects, from fresh produce to ethically reared meat. The Friday sourdough-pizza, BYO-booze nights here are nothing short of legendary.

To keep up with the local demand for 'real' bread (made without additives or chemicals), St Kew has launched a Cornish Bread Club from its micro-bakery. Following a similar model to well-known veg-box schemes, you select your loaf and collection day of choice, and your bread will be ready for you, fresh from the oven.

Within the farm shop is a small, rustic café serving lunch and snacks. The butternut-squash soup, served with crusty bread and lashings of butter, is a popular choice. Don't forget to leave room for a brownie or two.

Specialities: bread, pizzas

Kernow Forno
Pop-up pizza

4
SERVICE

4
HEALTHY FOOD

3
AMBIENCE

See website for upcoming events

££

Various locations across Cornwall and the southwest
07824 325 633
www.kernowforno.co.uk

Getting There
For details of pop-up locations, see website.

The Secret
Try one of Kernow Forno's devilish dessert pizzas, which include banana and dark-chocolate chunks, apple crumble and clotted cream, and chocolate and balsamic strawberry.

If you like your pizza toppings on a thin and crispy base, you need to track down Kernow Forno on your West Country travels. This pop-up appears regularly at parties, festivals and other events across the region.

Each pizza is made from scratch using fresh, silky dough that's kneaded, shaped and then baked in a wood-fired oven on wheels. Set at a constant 450 degrees, the oven cooks pizzas in a matter of seconds. In fact, the team can make, bake and serve 70 pizzas an hour, which is quite something.

Toppings include roasted butternut squash with goat's cheese, pine nuts and rosemary, and a popular BLT option. Gluten-free bases are available and cooked on trays to avoid cross-contamination from the oven floor.

Specialities: Cornish salami and mozzarella, the dessert pizza

Rectory Farm Tea Rooms
More tea, vicar?

These award-winning tearooms, with their proximity to the footpath that stretches the length of the rugged Cornish coastline, are the perfect place for some rest and relaxation after a bracing stroll.

Come prepared for cakes, scones and jams galore. The selection of savoury bites on offer includes quiches, soups and pasties. All fish and meat is sourced locally and all salad and vegetables are picked from the owners' kitchen garden. There are gluten-free options on the menu, as well as nutritious children's dishes.

The building, which dates from the 13th century, is steeped in folklore. The oak beams in the tearooms are spoils from some of the many ships that have gone aground along this treacherous stretch of coast.

Specialities: afternoon tea, ploughman's lunches, Cornish pasties

Apr–Oct daily 11–5   ££

Crosstown, Morwenstow, Bude,
Cornwall EX23 9SR
01288 331 251
www.rectory-tearooms.co.uk

Getting There
Between Bideford and Bude on the A39, take the road to Morwenstow. The tearooms are next to the church.

The Secret
Over the last 25 years, tearoom owners Jill and Richard Savage have amassed an enormous collection of beautiful vintage china, which is available for hire.

5
SERVICE

4
HEALTHY
FOOD

5
AMBIENCE

COFFEE BAR

OWICHES · PASTIES

BBQ Inkies → ORDER HERE

Inkie's Smokehouse BBQ

SMOKED PIG £5
{ PULLED PORK IN A BRIOCHE BAP }

SMOKED COW £6·50
{ BEEF BRISKET IN A BRIOCHE BAP }

AUTHENTICALLY COOKED OVER **WOOD** & **CHARCOAL** FOR A MINIMUM OF **18** HOURS

HOT DOG

FAT DOG WITH ONION £4
DIRTY DOG DOG WITH PULLED PORK £5
PUPPY DOG JUST FOR THE KIDS £3
{ FREE REINDEER BISCUIT WITH EVERY KIDS PUPPY DOG }

DON'T FORGET TO SAUCE UP!

Inkie's Smokehouse BBQ
Cooked low & slow

5 SERVICE

5 HEALTHY FOOD

4 AMBIENCE

See website for upcoming events   ££

Various locations in Cornwall
07849 488 655
www.inkiessmokehousebbq.com

Getting There
For details of pop-up locations, see website.

The Secret
The slow-smoking process at Inkie's creates a visible 'smoke ring' on the outside of the meat and around the bones – a sign of well-cooked meat, despite its red colouring.

Inkie's Smokehouse BBQ has reinvigorated Cornwall's street-food scene, thanks to its pairing of beautifully cooked meat with punchy homemade sauces.

South Carolina vinegar sauce is said to be the original barbecue sauce, and when dashed generously over the slow-cooked pulled pork, it's a taste sensation. Delicious extras include home-grown chillies in the hot sauce, a top-secret herb and spice mix in the dry rub and the crunchiest slaw imaginable. Have a dollop of creamy mayo if you need to cool down all that spice.

Inkie's meat is locally sourced and smoked for 18 hours over hickory, maple, cherry or apple hardwoods. If you feel like going all out, then order a meat platter with corn bread, potato salad and slaw on the side.

Specialities: pulled pork and South Carolina vinegar meat platter, slaw

Riverford
Home of the veg box

Guy Watson, founder of Riverford, started growing organic vegetables on a few acres back in 1986. In the early days, he delivered veg boxes to around 30 friends in Devon – a far cry from the 47,000 homes in the UK that now receive a weekly box from one of Riverford's four regional farms.

The farm shop at Riverford's headquarters in Devon, Wash Farm, sells a staggering range of fresh produce, as well as many household staples. The butcher's counter is brimming with locally reared, organic meats.

While you're here, have lunch at the excellent on-site Field Kitchen Restaurant and then burn it off on a self-guided farm walk. Simply grab a map, an MP3 player – which gives interesting snippets from Guy about the route and the farm – and a pair of wellies.

Speciality: fresh, seasonal, organic meat and veg

Mon–Sat 9–6, Sun 10–5   ££

Wash Farm, Buckfastleigh, Devon
TQ11 0JU, 01803 762 059
www.riverford.co.uk

Getting There
From Buckfastleigh, take the Totnes road (A384). Take the third exit on the left (after approx 2.5km) and then follow the signs to Riverford Organics.

The Secret
For a taste of Riverford in the heart of the city, visit The Duke of Cambridge in Islington, London – this pub uses produce from Riverford farms and suppliers.

5
SERVICE

5
HEALTHY FOOD

4
AMBIENCE

Seadog
On the road again

4 SERVICE

5 HEALTHY FOOD

2 AMBIENCE

See website for upcoming events

£

Various locations in Devon
07475 436 819
www.seadogfoods.co.uk

Getting There
For details of pop-up locations, see website.

The Secret
Book Seadog to cater at a private event, and expect something out of the ordinary, from Lord of the Rings-themed feasts to campfire catering. Quirky and very cool.

The Seadog kitchen trailer, which is run by two chefs, plies its trade along the North Devon coast. The menu is inspired by world food, using ingredients from local traders and growers. All herbs are home-grown and all fish is locally landed and sustainably caught.

The dishes served up in the Seadog trailer reflect the owners' passion for travel (and local seafood!), accounting for the Devon seafood lasagne, Thai beef curry, Goan chickpea and spinach curry, Bolivian chilli beef and Jamaican fish pasties. The menu, like the trailer's location, is forever changing, depending on what's available from the market each day.

Seadog represents the very best in West Country street food, and you get to enjoy it in the most spectacular coastal settings. What more could you want?

Specialities: global cuisine, homemade cakes

Darts Farm
Meat-lovers unite

(4) SERVICE

(4) HEALTHY FOOD

(5) AMBIENCE

Mon–Sat 8–7,
Sun 9.30–4.30

£££

Topsham, Exeter, Devon EX3 0QH
01392 878 200
www.dartsfarm.co.uk

Getting There
From Exeter, take the A376 towards
Exmouth. Turn off towards Topsham,
and Darts Farm is on your right.

The Secret
*Darts Farm won Best Independent
Food Shop in the* Devon Life *awards
and appeared in* BBC Good Food
*magazine's top ten UK farm shops,
among many other accolades.*

Forty years ago, Darts Farm was nothing more than a
small hut selling fruit and vegetables at the bottom of
a field; today, it's a gigantic food hub. According to
The Guardian, walking inside is 'like finding Selfridges
food hall dumped in the middle of a field'. And it's easy to
see why, with masses of exquisite produce at every turn.

The food is divided into different sections, including a
butcher, fishmonger, deli counter, greengrocer, cider
works and alehouse. But it's the skilled butchers who
really steal the show, with their regular meat master
classes, including a Christmas session that teaches you
how to bone and roll a turkey.

There's plenty to occupy kids here, with farm trails,
bike-hire facilities and a maze (made from maize). The
chefs in the restaurant use the food hall as their larder.

Specialities: farm-reared Red Ruby beef, sausages

Oasis Falafel and Grill
Favourite falafels

4
SERVICE

4
HEALTHY FOOD

3
AMBIENCE

Generally 10.30–5 in the week, but times can vary

£

Guildhall Shopping Centre, Exeter, Devon EX4 3HP, 07786 157 734
www.facebook.com/OasisFalafelGrill

Getting There
The shopping centre is adjacent to Exeter High Street. For details of pop-up locations, see website.

The Secret
According to many local fans, these are the best falafels on earth – high praise indeed given this foodstuff originated in the Middle East.

The satisfyingly crisp falafels dished out at this authentic Egyptian street-food stall have the perfect balance of spices, imported directly from North Africa. Made every day from a fresh chickpea mix, the falafels are cooked and served in a wrap with salad, tahini and hot sauce. Watch out for the hottest hot sauce – it packs a real punch.

Not only are queues for Oasis generally quite long (especially at festivals), but the cooking cannot be rushed, so be prepared to wait for your food – and it's worth it.

You'll find Oasis Falafel and Grill in the Guildhall Shopping Centre in Exeter, but it's wise to check the Facebook page for opening times, which are quite changeable, and for details of pop-up events.

Specialities: falafel, beef shawarma

Felicity's Farm Shop
Food with a view

Felicity's Farm Shop overlooks the National Trust Golden Cap estate, which is situated on the coast between Bridport and Charmouth. Can there be a farm shop anywhere else in the UK with a finer view than this? We're willing to wager not.

Inside, you'll find an impressive range of food, including fresh produce, local cheeses, breads, pastries, rare-breed meats and the daily catch, landed at nearby Bridport. On the wall next to the butcher's fridges, a sign indicates the provenance of all the meat on sale, including the distance it has travelled – a nice touch.

If you're feeling flush, this is a dream venue for a weekly shop. Otherwise, it's a great place to come for a snack and a coffee at the Filling Station Café before browsing the groceries, home- and kitchenware, toys and gifts.

Specialities: locally reared pork, local honey

Mon–Sat 9–5, Sun 10–4   ££

Morcombelake, Devon DT6 6DJ
01297 480 930
www.felicitysfarmshop.co.uk

Getting There
Heading west on the A35 from Bridport to Axminster, you'll find Felicity's Farm Shop on the left-hand side, with remarkable views of Dorset and out to sea.

The Secret
Due to popular demand, Felicity's now stocks a gluten-free, organic real ale. Masquerade is made by award-winning Monty's Brewery in Powys, Wales.

5
SERVICE

5
HEALTHY FOOD

4
AMBIENCE

Downhouse Farm Garden Café
The birds and the bees

5
SERVICE

5
HEALTHY FOOD

5
AMBIENCE

Mar–end Oct Tue–Sun 10–6

££

Higher Eype, Bridport, Dorset DT6 6AH, 01308 421 232
www.downhousefarm.org

Getting There
On the coast path between Eype and Seatown, you'll see signs to the farm. From the A35, turn onto Higher Eype Road and then left at the farm sign.

The Secret
If you fall in love with Downhouse Farm, consider booking its cosy shepherd's hut for the night – simply open the stable door to enjoy smashing sea views.

Hidden away on the National Trust Golden Cap estate, Downhouse Farm Garden Café is one of those places you're unlikely to stumble upon by chance. But it's worth hunting down, especially if you're in need of some time out during a long day on your feet.

The café is very pretty, and at the height of summer, the garden is a mass of moving colour, thanks to the wildflowers, butterflies, birds and bees. Beyond the lovely covered area, there are jaw-dropping views of the Eype Downs, which are carpeted in bluebells in May.

Part of a working farm, this café is the ideal place for dog walkers and ramblers to stop for a tasty daily special or a freshly baked scone and jam. Afterwards, you're encouraged to explore the many meandering footpaths that crisscross the farm.

Specialities: cream teas, spicy lentil daal

Rachel's
A kiosk with a view

5
SERVICE

5
HEALTHY FOOD

4
AMBIENCE

Midday–3.30 (dependent on weather and season)   £

3 The Mound, West Bay, Dorset
DT6 4HA, 07974 314 277

Getting There
Rachel's is one of the wooden food shacks on the southwest side of Bridport Harbour.

The Secret
Rachel's serves up a refreshing take on an old pub favourite – its fisherman's ploughman's features fresh crab, prawns, homemade smoked-mackerel pâté, a boiled-egg salad and a hunk of crusty bread.

Perched on West Bay quayside, Rachel's boasts great views out over the harbour towards Bridport. It may be nothing fancy to look at, but this kiosk serves huge portions of the freshest seafood, cooked perfectly and sold at reasonable prices. Such is the huge popularity of this place, it's common to see punters queuing up for lunch as late as 3 o'clock in the afternoon.

Despite the rather humdrum name, the fish stew is exquisite, with its mix of local seafood served in a rich tomato broth with crusty bread. The simply prepared shellfish plucked straight from the sea speaks for itself.

Although there's no indoor seating at Rachel's, there's plenty of room outside on shared wooden picnic tables. It gets very busy, especially in the high season, but you're always told how long the wait is likely to be.

Specialities: fish stew, scallops, crab salad

Eweleaze Farm
Carry on camping

4

SERVICE

4

HEALTHY
FOOD

5

AMBIENCE

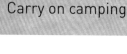
Summer daily 8–9

£

Osmington, Dorset DT3 6ED
01305 833 690
www.eweleaze.co.uk

Getting There
From Weymouth, take the A354 north
towards Dorchester. Turn right onto
the A353 and the farm is on your right,
opposite the White Horse hill figure.

The Secret
*Eweleaze offers so much more than
regular campsites – expect retro
folding campers and stylish bell tents
for hire, and wood-fired saunas.*

In August every year, the small, organic Eweleaze Farm
opens its gates and turns from a bucolic coastal farm
into a buzzing, family-friendly campsite.

At the farm shop, you can buy meat from Aberdeen
Angus cattle reared on pasture and organic fruit and
vegetables from local suppliers, as well as the more
mundane camping essentials. The bakery offers all
kinds of breads and pastries, and contains a hot-food
canteen. And then there's a pizza van that turns out a
range of pizzas straight from the oven.

Once at Eweleaze, it's tempting not to get in the car till
home time: here, good food is only ever a short walk
away and you're given access to a private beach where
friendly goats and ponies roam free.

Specialities: pizzas, Aberdeen Angus steaks and
burgers

The Udder Farm Shop
A rural delight

SERVICE 4

HEALTHY FOOD 4

AMBIENCE 3

Mon–Fri 9–6, Sat 8.30–6, Sun 9.30–4   ££

Manor Farm, East Stour, Gillingham, Dorset SP8 5LQ, 01747 838 899
www.theudderfarmshop.co.uk

Getting There
Heading along the A30 from Shaftesbury to Sherborne, the shop is on your left.

The Secret
Monthly recipes on the farm-shop website give fascinating facts about ingredients: did you know, for example, that a recipe for cooking asparagus appears in the world's oldest cookbook, which dates from the 4th century AD?

The award-winning Udder Farm Shop, with its fantastic butchery and deli, offers a refreshing alternative to supermarket shopping – if your wallet allows, that is.

Most of the beef and pork here comes from neighbouring Down Farm – which is owned by the same people who own the farm shop – while the fresh fruit and vegetables, eggs and cheeses are all locally sourced. At the deli counter, expect quiches, terrines, Scotch eggs and large bowls of spice mixtures. The farm shop is also known for its wide selection of high-quality, homemade ready meals, as nutritious as they are delicious.

There's also a fully licensed, on-site restaurant here, which is open for breakfast and lunch throughout the week. The full English breakfasts are excellent.

Specialities: Down Farm beef, cheese scones, mixed spices, Sunday roast (in the restaurant)

Barford Ice Cream Garden
Sorbet & sunshine

5

SERVICE

3

HEALTHY
FOOD

5

AMBIENCE

Apr–Sep Tue–Sun
11.30–5.30

£

Barford Farm, Sturminster
Marshall, Wimborne, Dorset
BH21 4BY, 01258 857 969
www.barford-icecream.co.uk

Getting There
Barford Farm is on the lane linking
Sturminster Marshall and Wimborne
Minster. The ice-cream garden is very
well signposted.

The Secret
*If you have access to a nearby freezer,
you can take away a 0.5- or 1-litre tub
of your favourite flavour to enjoy later.*

Barford Ice Cream Garden is situated near the River
Stour on the National Trust Kingston Lacy estate. It's a
magical place with secret hideaways for kids to explore
and plenty of seating – try to find a spot in the dappled
shade of an old weeping willow or oak tree.

And now to the real reason you've come here: the
delicious ice cream, which is sold from a wooden shed
behind the farmhouse. Made from the milk of the
Jersey cows you can see in the very next field, it comes
in some unusual flavours, including Christmas pudding,
liquorice and the yukky-sounding, yummy-tasting
'farmyard slurry'. Children's size and gluten-free cones
are available, as are ice creams for diabetics.

Call ahead if you're making a special visit, as it closes
in bad weather. Parking and garden entry are free.

Specialities: Christmas pudding and liquorice flavours

The Steak Out
Cute & carniverous

Dreamed up by a team of committed festival-goers who mourned the absence of top-quality British food among the countless world-food stalls at the events they frequented, the Steak Out celebrates all things local – no grubby old burgers here!

Steaks are made using high-quality meat from pasture-reared Somerset cattle, cheese comes from producers across the county and salads are bought at the local market.

The ever-popular Classic is a fresh roll stuffed to the gunnels with rump steak and topped with fried onions, while the Steak Out is a more decadent version of the same, served with cheese. It's a Wrap is ideal for those who like the meat to do the talking, with a thin tortilla wrap replacing the plump bread roll.

Speciality: steak

Mon–Wed 8–5,
Thu–Sat 8–9

££

Various locations in Dorset
01425 628 589
www.thesteakoutpod.co.uk

Getting There
For details of pop-up locations, see website.

The Secret
Painted on the outside with a highly decorative version of the Union Jack and with fresh flowers on the counter, The Steak Out's catering pod has to be one of the prettiest in the southwest.

4
SERVICE

3
HEALTHY FOOD

3
AMBIENCE

The Bristol Sausage Shop
A Bristol institution

5
SERVICE

4
HEALTHY FOOD

4
AMBIENCE

Mon–Sat 10–4

 £

28–30 The Glass Arcade, St Nicholas Market, Bristol BS1 1LJ
07817 478 302

Getting There
This is one of many food vendors in the Glass Arcade at St Nicholas Market, just off Corn Street, to the north of Bristol Old Vic theatre.

The Secret
An amazing 98% of the ingredients used in these sausages are local – and according to the owners, 'local' means within an hour's drive of the shop.

Whatever you look for in a good old British banger, this small shop with a big reputation is likely to have it. The bestseller is the traditional Gloucester Old Spot – a rare-breed sausage with a name that speaks for itself – but there are around twenty other creative combinations to sink your teeth into.

How about lamb, leek and rosemary for Sunday lunch, or beef and real ale with a Friday night pint? The pork, red onion and ginger is deliciously smoky, with a caramel sweetness, while The Lucifer answers the prayers of every chilli head out there, with its outrageous blend of pork and sizzling jalapeno peppers.

Order your sausage lunch to take away and buy half a dozen sausages for the freezer while you're here.

Specialities: Gloucester Old Spot, The Lucifer, beef and real-ale sausages

Eat a Pitta
A proper pitta

If queues are a good indication of the quality of food at a street stall, then you're in for a treat when you join the end of the line at Eat a Pitta.

The falafel served here, in the street-food hub known as St Nicholas Market, comes from a recipe that originated in the owner's grandmother's back-street Algerian kitchen more than 70 years ago. A tasty crust gives way to a moist, fragrant, herby centre – the perfect match for the crisp salad accompaniments.

Buy a handful of falafels as a snack, or tuck into an oversized pitta or salad box for lunch. These come packed with falafel, colourful salads, pickles, hummus, couscous and zingy homemade sauces. Freshly made throughout the day and at £4.50 a pop, these bigger portions have to be one of the city's best-value meals.

Specialities: falafel, hummus, fresh salads

Mon–Fri 11–4, Sat 11–5   £

1–3 Glass Arcade, St Nicholas Market, Bristol BS1 1LJ
07825 659 525
www.eatapitta.co.uk

Getting There
This is one of many food vendors in the Glass Arcade at St Nicholas Market, just off Corn Street, to the north of Bristol Old Vic theatre.

The Secret
Virtuous and versatile, the falafels served at Eat a Pitta are free from meat, dairy, gluten, eggs and nuts.

5
SERVICE

5
HEALTHY FOOD

4
AMBIENCE

The Better Food Company
The urban farm shop

G V ♿ 🏃

5

SERVICE

5

HEALTHY
FOOD

3

AMBIENCE

Mon–Fri 9–8, Sat 9–7,
Sun 10–6

££

94 Whiteladies Road, Bristol
BS8 2QX, 0117 946 6957
www.betterfood.co.uk

Getting There
Head to the north of the city on
Whiteladies Road (A4018) and The
Better Food Company is on your left,
at the junction with Hurle Road.

The Secret
*The Better Food Company sells a festival
survival kit, which contains viridian milk
thistle to combat over-indulgence, as
well as organic goodies and lotions.*

Urban farm shop, health-food store and deli rolled into
one, The Better Food Company aims to put the soul
back into household shopping. The ethos that drives
this pioneering brand – which has a bigger branch over
in St Werburghs – is far greater than profit alone. This is
a place that works hard to champion organic, local and
fair-trade products, while backing local and national
environmental schemes and community campaigns.

The shop's colourful fruit and veg aisles supply the
on-site juice bar, which makes up raw concoctions to
order. Grab one before exploring the bakery, with its
array of breads, cakes, pies and snacks, including some
delicious onion bhajis and samosas, and the food hall,
with its impressive range of organic wines, beers and
ethically sourced groceries.

Specialities: fruit and veg, Hobbs House Bread,
organic wines

Bath Farmers' Market
All under one roof

SERVICE 5

HEALTHY FOOD 4

AMBIENCE 5

Sat 9–1.30

 £ to ££

Green Park Station, Bath BA1 1JB
07779 697 278
www.bathfarmersmarket.co.uk

Getting There
The farmers' market takes place just off the A367 in Bath, at the renovated Green Park Station. From here, it's a short walk to Bath shopping centre.

The Secret
Bath Farmers' Market claims the title as the UK's first ever farmers' market, having first opened its doors back in 1997.

The stalls at Bath Farmers' Market overflow with the freshest and most wholesome produce from the local area. Expect all the usual suspects, from vibrant fruit and vegetables to artisan breads, pies and juices to the tenderest of meats. The Chaucer-inspired Wyfe of Bath cheese from the Bath Soft Cheese Company – a nutty, creamy, semi-hard cheese packed with the flavours of wildflowers and lush green meadows – comes highly recommended.

A stall to note is Lovett Pies, with its ham hock, black pudding and pea shortcrust-pastry pie. Among the meat stalls, be prepared for pigs' trotters and chicken gizzards. Although not everyone's cup of tea, these unsung animal parts can add an interesting dimension to your cooking and are much sought after among those who believe in nose-to-tail eating.

Specialities: Wyfe of Bath cheese, fresh wild game

Funghi Fruits
Mushroom Mecca

With Funghi Fruits, we're talking about food feet rather than food miles. Visionary owner Hugh Prentice has turned the disused vaults beneath Bath Farmers' Market into an oyster-mushroom farm, and it has to be one of the most sustainable food businesses around.

So how does it work? Hugh tours the city by bicycle or on foot, collecting waste coffee grounds from cafés. He impregnates each bag of waste coffee with oyster-mushroom spores and hangs them up in the controlled cellar environment. Just six weeks later, they're ready for harvesting and sold at the farmers' market and to local restaurants and veg-box providers. Hugh's aim is to make Bath 'self-sufficient in mushrooms'.

At the time of going to print, the growing rooms were out of bounds to visitors, although this might change.

Speciality: oyster mushrooms

Sat 8.30–1.30   £

Bath Farmers' Market, Green Park Station, Bath BA1 1JB
07966 080 005
www.fungifruits.org

Getting There
Fughi Fruits mushrooms are on sale at a stall at Bath Farmers' Market, which is just off the A367 in Bath.

The Secret
Grow-your-own boxes are on offer at this market stall. If you follow the instructions, your earthy wonders should sprout within seven days.

5
SERVICE

5
HEALTHY FOOD

4
AMBIENCE

Somerset Cider Brandy Company
Nectar of the Gods

5 SERVICE

3 HEALTHY FOOD

5 AMBIENCE

Mon–Sat 9–5.30

££

Pass Vale Farm, Kingsbury
Episcopi, Martock, Somerset
TA12 6BU, 01460 240 782
www.ciderbrandy.co.uk

Getting There
Go southwest towards Burrow from
the village of Kingsbury Episcopi. The
farm will be on your left-hand side.

The Secret
*Another way to enjoy the fruits of
SCBC's labours is at Glastonbury
Festival, from a bus next to the
Pyramid stage. Let the cider flow!*

Cider aficionados, brandy-lovers and rural historians
will benefit from a visit to the Somerset Cider Brandy
Company (SCBC). Getting lost en route seems par for
the course when visiting for the first time, but persevere
– it's well worth the effort.

This farm has been pressing cider for the past 150 years
and distilling cider brandy since 1989. In fact, the SCBC
led the revival of this rural art, which is mentioned in
written records that date back as early as 1678.

Depending on the season, you may catch a glimpse of
brandy being distilled, apples being picked and cider
being pressed, fermented and bottled. Visit the shop
and wander through the apple orchard, either on your
own or as part of an organised orchard trail, where the
tree-to-bottle process is fully explained.

Specialities: cider brandy, cider

Pitney Farm Shop
Free-range fun

PITNEY FARM SHOP

5

SERVICE

5

HEALTHY FOOD

5

AMBIENCE

Mon, Tue & Thu–Sat
9–5.30

£

Glebe Farm, Woodbirds Hill Lane,
Pitney, Langport, Somerset
TA10 9AP, 01458 253 002
www.pitneyfarmshop.co.uk

Getting There
From Pitney, head north onto Church
Hill and at the crossroads, turn left
onto Woodbirds Hill Lane. The farm is
a little way down on your right.

The Secret
*If you come here on foot, by bike or on
horseback, you get 5 per cent off the
bill for helping to save the planet.*

An idyllic scene awaits you at Pitney Farm Shop,
where chickens chase bugs in the yard and cats doze
on picnic tables. But behind this sleepy veneer is a hive
of industry where Saddleback sows and native breeds of
beef cattle are reared for meat and around 70 varieties
of organic vegetables are grown throughout the year.

It might be compact, but the farm shop stocks a wide
range of products. Outside the entrance is a little
wooden shed where home-grown fruit and vegetables
are sold. Inside, as well as Pitney's own home-reared
meat, you'll find freshly delivered organic breads,
pastries, preserves, chocolates and Somerset cheeses,
as well as local ciders and juices.

Combine a visit to this Soil Association-licensed
producer with one of the popular lambing open days.

Specialities: vegetables, burgers, sausages

Kimbers' Farm Shop
Happy meat

The Kimber family, which has run this farm for the last 300 years, puts a huge emphasis on animal welfare. With its mixed herd of Aberdeen Angus, shorthorn and Red Ruby cattle grazing on the lush pastures of Blackmore Vale, you can rest assured that the quality of the meat on sale in the shop is as high as can be.

As well as cattle, the family rears Gloucester Old Spots, producing roasting joints, sausages, chops and all manner of charcuterie, including smoked carpaccio of beef. You'll also find wild game, local poultry, lamb and dairy products, and everything else you'd expect from a farm shop worth its salt.

The Kimbers rely on the expertise of small local slaughterhouses and practice proper hanging methods to produce the most flavourful, tender meat.

Specialities: rose veal, chorizo, sausages

Tue–Fri 8.30–6.30, Sat 10–4   ££

Charlton Musgrove, Wincanton, Somerset BA9 8HD, 01963 33177
www.kimbersfarmshop.co.uk

Getting There
Kimbers' Farm Shop is easily located on the B3081 between Wincanton and Bruton.

The Secret
If you're planning a barbecue, picnic or big breakfast, you can order a meat box from the farm shop to be delivered straight to your door; choose a ready-made box by theme or by price, or build your own.

4
SERVICE

4
HEALTHY FOOD

3
AMBIENCE

Lye Cross Farm Shop
All aboard the café bus

5

SERVICE

4

HEALTHY FOOD

4

AMBIENCE

Mon–Fri 8–6, Sat 8–5,
Sun 10–4

£

Redhill, Somerset BS40 5RH
01934 864 600
www.lyecrossfarm.co.uk

Getting There
Heading south out of Bristol on the A38, the farm shop can be found just over 3km south of Bristol airport.

The Secret
Lye Cross Farm churns out a massive 6,000 tonnes of cheese a year for shipping around the world to such diverse locations as Saudi Arabia, Singapore and the Republic of Ireland.

The Alvis family, which has farmed the land here for 400 years, has been making cheese on site since 1952. Today, they combine traditional cheese-making methods, such as 'cheddaring' – turning and stacking the curd by hand – alongside cutting-edge technology, before aging the roundels for up to 18 months in a dairy just metres from the farm-shop tills.

Expect a fantastic choice of handmade and organic cheeses in the farm shop, as well as deli items, baked goods and fresh fruit and vegetables from the market.

Situated just off the A38, Lye Cross Farm is the ideal place to break up a long journey to the West Country. While you're here, jump aboard Dot the café bus for a cuppa or something from the simple menu – the cream teas are a great pick-me-up.

Specialities: cheeses, cream teas

Cookery Schools

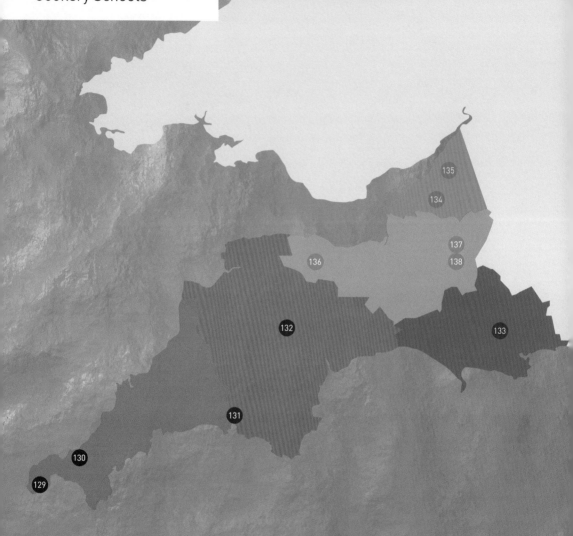

Southwest England
Cookery Schools

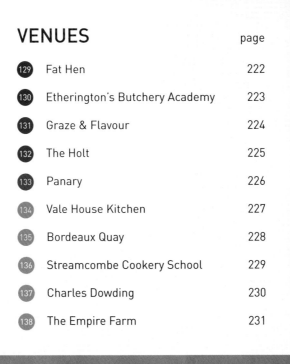

VENUES

		page
129	Fat Hen	222
130	Etherington's Butchery Academy	223
131	Graze & Flavour	224
132	The Holt	225
133	Panary	226
134	Vale House Kitchen	227
135	Bordeaux Quay	228
136	Streamcombe Cookery School	229
137	Charles Dowding	230
138	The Empire Farm	231

Fat Hen
Fancy a forage?

Gwenmenhir, Boscawen-noon Farm, St Buryan,
Penzance, Cornwall TR19 6EH, 01736 810 156
www.fathen.org

Getting There
Head west on the A30 from Penzance. Boscawen-noon
Farm is clearly marked on your left-hand side, about
1.5km beyond the hamlet of Catchall.

Our favourite class:	Seaweed Foraging & Cookery
Maximum class size:	12
Meals included:	Lunch
Class cost:	£95

The Secret
*This cookery school is named after a spinach-like edible
plant, not a breed of poultry; fat hen was a staple crop
2,000 years ago, but is now generally treated as a weed.*

The courses at the Fat Hen have three distinct stages:
foraging, cooking and feasting. To start with, you'll
head out into the wilds of Cornwall with a foraging
expert to pick up everything from watercress and
woodland mushrooms to samphire and seaweed.

Back in the school kitchen, professional chefs will
show you how to turn nature's humblest ingredients
into a delicious three-course feast, which you'll enjoy
by candlelight with other course members at long
farmhouse tables in a former goat barn.

If you think Fat Hen – which has been recommended
by both BBC *Countryfile* and *The Telegraph* – sounds
like fun, it's wise to book up one of its popular courses
before everyone else does. Choose from Seaweed
Foraging & Cookery, Fish & Shellfish Cookery, Game
Cookery, Wild Italian Cookery, Artisan Bread Making or
an epic Gourmet Wild Food Weekend, among others.

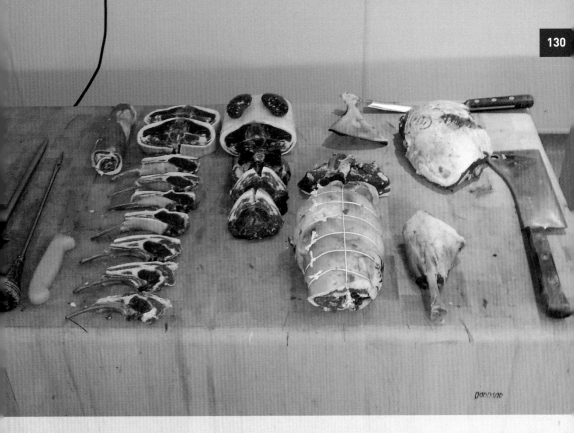

Etherington's Butchery Academy
Mastering meat

Etherington's hands-on butchery courses make great gifts for anyone who loves their food and wants to know more about where it comes from. Although the focus on nose-to-tail eating might put off those with squeamish tendencies, it provides a full and fascinating overview of the basics of this age-old skill.

Drawing on 60 years of meaty know-how, the team will teach you a range of techniques, including knife-handling, posture and tying the notorious 'butcher's knot'. You'll also tackle the rather intimidating job of dissecting a carcass into different cuts and joints. Reassuringly, all the beef, pork, lamb, turkey and chicken prepared here can be traced to a local farm.

At the end of these half-day and day-long courses, students take away a butchery kit to help get them started in the kitchen, as well as some sample cuts of meat they have butchered on the day.

Wheal Rose, Scorrier, Redruth, Cornwall
TR16 5DF, 01209 899 203
www.etherington-meats.co.uk

Getting There
Etherington's is situated in the village of Wheal Rose, near Scorrier, just off the A30, about 3km northeast of Redruth.

Our favourite class:	Pig Butchery & Sausage Making
Maximum class size:	8
Meals included:	A light lunch
Class cost:	£70

The Secret
Etherington's takes sustainable living seriously, from the higher-welfare meat it sources to the solar panels on the roof to the building itself, crafted from local stone.

Graze & Flavour
Foodie adventures

Day starts off in Plymouth, Devon
07906 015 513
www.grazeandflavour.co.uk

Getting There
Plymouth is located just off the A38 – the Devon
Expressway. You'll be given more information on
locations nearer to the time of your course.

Our favourite class:	F.I.S.H trail
Maximum class size:	18
Meals included:	Catch of the day
Class cost:	£140

The Secret
*Did you know that a mackerel's dark top and light belly
camouflage it from above and below? Just one of many
fun facts you'll pick up on a course with Graze & Flavour.*

Whether you're after a structured course, a bespoke
food and drink trail or a business-bonding event,
Graze & Flavour aims to find 'the people, stories and
landscapes behind the ingredients on your plate'.

You'll start the popular F.I.S.H trail with a tour of
Plymouth's fish market before venturing out onto
the high seas with a rod and line to catch your lunch.
Landlubbers might prefer Hog & Grog, which involves
butchering a side of pork, brewing a '6-hour beer',
smoking pork and making chorizo – no mean feat for
a day-long course! And, as part of the Coffee Cupping,
you'll learn about coffees from such diverse places as
Sumatra, Ethiopia, Peru and Devon.

Serious food-lovers, though, are likely to be drawn to
the Tastes of Topsham gourmet weekend. Over these
two days, you'll meet artisan food and drink producers
from across Devon, and sample their delicious produce.

The Holt
I'm cured

There's rather a lot of information out there on how to smoke and cure foods, but when it comes to preserving meats, it's really important to get it right. A good grounding in the theory, method and science behind this somewhat daunting practice of food preservation is absolutely essential.

The courses at The Holt, a popular Honiton pub, cover all the basics necessary to set you up with your own personal production line of cured and smoked foods. Learn about hot- and cold-smoking techniques, as well as different curing methods and when to use them, the importance of brine strengths and ratios, and the role of salt and sugar in the curing process.

Expect a sociable two-hour class that revolves around tastings and discussions rather than hands-on work. And if it gets you in the mood for learning, you can always sign up to do a bread class next.

178 High Street, Honiton, Devon EX14 1LA
01404 477 07
www.theholt-honiton.com

Getting There
The market town of Honiton lies just south of the A30, about 35km outside Exeter. The Holt, located on Honiton High Street, couldn't be easier to find.

Our favourite class:	Beginner's Smoking & Curing
Maximum class size:	12
Meals included:	Tasting
Class cost:	£30

The Secret
Expect a free pint of local Otter beer on a course here – The Holt owners, Joe and Angus McCaig, are part of the family behind Devon's much-loved Otter Brewery.

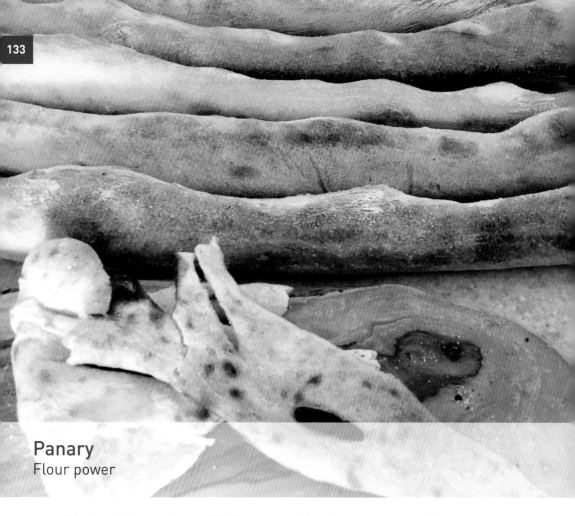

Panary
Flour power

Cann Mills, Cann, Shaftesbury, Dorset SP7 0BL
01747 823 711
www.panary.co.uk

Getting There
Located on the A358, halfway between the A303 and
Blandford Forum, Panary is refreshingly easy to get
to. Just look out for the signs.

Our favourite class:	1-Day Wood-Fired Oven
Maximum class size:	6
Meals included:	Lunch
Class cost:	£175

The Secret
*Panary occupies part of Cann Mills, a working watermill,
which produces a growing range of organic stoneground
flours that are used in all bread-making courses here.*

Browsing through the long list of courses on Panary's
website, you might find it hard to pick just one. If
you're stuck, we recommend you go for the day-long
Wood-Fired Oven course, which offers a superb insight
into the workings of a masonry wood-fired oven and is
a great all-round option for beginners.

Led by Paul Merry – an artisan baker for more than
40 years, a bread-making tutor for 20 and the brains
behind Panary – you'll learn how to bake everything
from focaccia to *baladi* flatbread. And, as the oven
cools throughout the day, you'll rake out the coals and
ashes and cook meats, vegetables, casseroles and
puddings on the oven floor.

Other courses at Panary include learning about the
process of yeast fermentation, British bread types and
techniques, fancy rustic shapes from France and Italy,
and sourdough and pizza best practice.

Vale House Kitchen
From field to fork

Vale House Kitchen is not just a cookery school – it's also a place to learn country skills, from fishing and foraging to shooting, brewing and butchery. So, as well as the more mainstream chutney- and bread-making courses you might expect from a reputable school, be prepared to don your wellies and barber and head out into the surrounding countryside to find, catch or shoot the food that will end up on your plate.

The two-day Shooting Experience is an eye-opener for anyone who's new to the field-to-fork philosophy. It encompasses everything from gun-safety to shooting, preparing and cooking game using traditional and contemporary techniques.

At Vale House Kitchen, classes never exceed 8–10 people, involve both demonstrations and hands-on elements, and are led by award-winning tutors in a state-of-the-art on-site kitchen.

Loves Hill, Timsbury, Bath BA2 0EU
01761 470 401
www.valehousekitchen.co.uk

Getting There
Vale House Kitchen is located in the village of Timsbury, just 12km outside Bath, between the city and the Mendip HIlls.

Our favourite class:	The Shooting Experience
Maximum class size:	10–12
Meals included:	Lunch
Class cost:	£60

The Secret
Chef and head tutor, Tim Maddams, has some impressive credentials, having worked with everyone from Marco Pierre White to the Ferrari F1 and River Cottage teams.

Bordeaux Quay
Blade runner

V-Shed, Canons Way, Bristol BS1 5UH
0117 943 1200
www.bordeaux-quay.co.uk

Getting There
This cookery school is located slap-bang in the centre of the city, near to the At-Bristol science centre and the harbour.

Our favourite class:	Knife Skills
Maximum class size:	13
Meals included:	Supper
Class cost:	£60

The Secret
Bordeaux Quay offers a range of kids' cookery courses in the school holidays, as well as themed birthday parties such as The Great British Tea Party.

The choice of cookery workshops at Bordeaux Quay is nothing short of staggering. Whether you want to know more about preparing meat and fish, making bread, pasta, preserves and patisserie, using spices more confidently or matching tapas dishes to different Spanish wines, this kitchen leaves very few gastronomic stones unturned.

But if we had to pick just one course for a novice chef to begin with, we'd suggest knife skills, which underpins so many culinary activities. On this evening class, under the watchful eye of an experienced tutor, you'll learn the best way to sharpen your knife, as well as how to slice, dice, chop, *brunoise* (create very small cubes) and *julienne* (create batons).

Your newfound knowledge will be put to good use straight away, as you prepare a simple two-course supper to be enjoyed at the end of the class.

Streamcombe Cookery School
Ahead of the game

This cookery school, located in an ancient stone barn just south of Exmoor, offers a wide range of bespoke, private, group, team-building and party courses on a spectrum of food themes.

For those who want to learn how to prepare and cook game, the class at Streamcombe will get you off to a flying start, with advice on working with rabbit, partridge, pheasant and venison. You'll also get the chance to forage for ingredients in the nearby fields and hedgerows to make your dishes even wilder.

Wild meat is so different from the mass-produced, packaged products that fill supermarket shelves, it deserves a different approach in the kitchen. And that's exactly what this course offers.

Chef, owner and course tutor, Ian, has cooked for some big food names, including Prue Leith and Jamie Oliver.

Streamcombe Farm, Dulverton, Somerset
TA22 9SA, 01398 322 873
www.streamcombecookery.co.uk

Getting There
Dulverton is situated on the southern border of Exmoor National Park. Take Cottage Lane south out of town and you'll come across Streamcombe Farm.

Our favourite class:	Game & Seasonal Inspiration
Maximum class size:	6
Meals included:	Lunch
Class cost:	£125

The Secret
Bed and breakfast accommodation is available here, in the lovely stone barn or the cosy shepherd's hut in the garden – and it's discounted for cookery-school students.

Charles Dowding
Reap what you sow

Homeacres, Alhampton, Shepton Mallet, Somerset
BA4 6PZ, 01749 860 292
www.charlesdowding.co.uk

Getting There
Alhampton is a hamlet roughly 10km south of
the Mendip Hills. Approach via the A303, the A37
or the A361.

Our favourite class:	Homeacres Day Course
Maximum class size:	10–12
Meals included:	Lunch
Class cost:	£95

The Secret
*Charles experiments with the concept of moon sowing –
this doesn't mean sowing by moonlight, but during certain
phases of the moon, in order to achieve a bigger harvest.*

Meet Charles Dowding, a master of the art of no-dig
gardening – a skill he has perfected over 30 years.
Here, in his intensive market garden, he cultivates
fresh fruit and vegetables for local restaurants and
shops using a no-tillage, weeding-light approach.

On the Homeacres Day Course, you'll cover everything
you need to know about keeping the soil clear of
weeds and the different composts and manures
that are available, as well as how to make your
own compost. You'll be taken through simple steps
to improve your sowing and growing techniques,
receiving advice on everything from slug control to
buying your own polytunnel.

You'll come away brimming with ideas for your patch
of ground, whatever its size, and probably a whole load
of mouthwatering mental images of the meals your
bumper harvest will make.

The Empire Farm
Back to basics

If you shoot or have a friendly gamekeeper ready to drop off the odd brace of pheasants on your doorstep, you're likely to find the highly practical Wild Meats Butchery & Charcuterie course at The Empire Farm very useful indeed.

You'll learn everything you need to know about turning your catch into a splendid family meal, from plucking a bird to skinning and jointing a rabbit. You'll also be shown how a deer carcass is skinned. Afterwards, there are demonstrations on cooking, curing, sausage-making, meat-potting and game-buying techniques. Summer courses usually include venison, rabbit, hare, pigeon or squirrel, while in winter, you can expect venison, pheasant or partridge.

Other courses cover lamb and pork butchery, cider-making, the art of the three-bird roast and how to live the good life on less than an acre.

Throop Road, Templecombe, Somerset BA8 0HR
01963 371 681
www.empirefarm.co.uk

Getting There
The village of Templecombe is a few kilometres south of the A303, between Illchester and Mere, and the cookery school is just a stone's throw from the railway station.

Our favourite class:	Wild Meats Butchery & Charcuterie
Maximum class size:	12
Meals included:	Lunch and tastings to take home
Class cost:	£130

The Secret
It's thought there was once a tunnel from the wine cellar to the church at the end of the lane – the farm's gamekeeper claims to have played in it as a boy. The search is on!

Foodie Towns

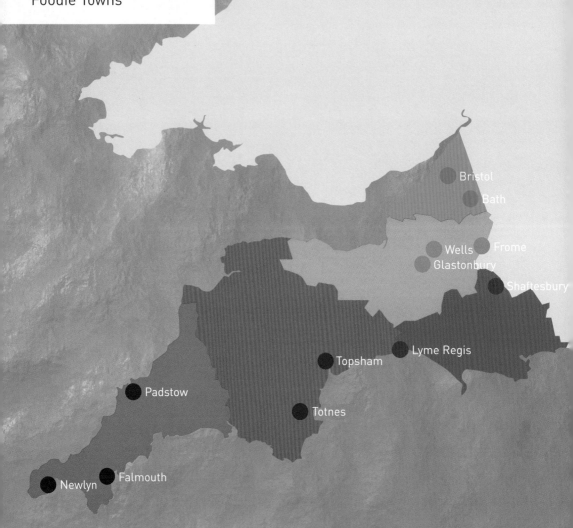

Southwest England
Foodie Towns

Bristol

Bath

Wells

Frome

Glastonbury

Shaftesbury

Lyme Regis

Topsham

Padstow

Totnes

Newlyn

Falmouth

TOWNS

		page
●	Newlyn	237
●	Falmouth	237
●	Padstow	237
●	Totnes	239
●	Topsham	239
●	Lyme Regis	241
●	Shaftesbury	241
●	Bristol	243
●	Bath	243
●	Glastonbury	245
●	Wells	245
●	Frome	245

Cornwall
Foodie Towns

Surrounded by the clean, cool waters of the Atlantic and the English Channel, Cornwall is renowned – above all – for its delicious, diverse seafood, available at markets and restaurants across the county. Even fish and chip shops here serve up beautifully fresh fish, which has often been landed that very same morning.

But no rundown of Cornish food would be complete without a mention of the humble Cornish pasty. Traditionally made with beef, potato, swede and plenty of seasoning, these parcels come in all kinds of creative varieties, from tandoori chicken to apple and blackberry.

Newlyn

It's no surprise that there are so many seafood restaurants in and around Newlyn – one of the most prolific fishing ports in the UK. This small town is also home to the Old Pilchard Works Museum, which celebrates the trade and tradition upon which the community was built.

Falmouth

The university town of Falmouth has a young and hip population that demands out-of-the-ordinary food. You'll find a heap of independent eateries here, including a vegan café called Wildebeest (see p.22) that deserves a special mention for its imaginative menu.

Padstow

Dubbed 'Padstein' by the locals ever since celebrity chef Rick Stein opened a handful of establishments here, Padstow is no secret. But that doesn't make it any less impressive for a visiting food fanatic. Pick and choose between the countless cafés, delis and restaurants that pepper this seaside town, and plan a visit to the National Lobster Hatchery, which safeguards lobster stocks in the UK and beyond.

Devon
Foodie Towns

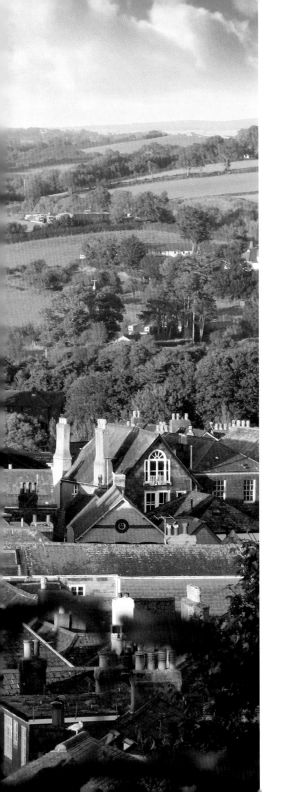

The largely rural county of Devon, which is home to the wilds of Dartmoor and Exmoor, is known for its fantastic array of regional cattle and pig breeds. And on menus across the county, these older, more traditional breeds are making a comeback, which is good news if you're after a flavourful meat feast. The ancient Red Ruby breed of cattle – famous in the culinary world for the beautiful marbling and succulence of its meat – is just such a breed.

And then there's the world-famous Devon cream tea, which – according to tradition – involves spreading clotted cream thickly on top of a scone, before topping the lot with lashings of strawberry jam. Controversially, it's done the other way round in Cornwall.

Totnes

Totnes hit the headlines when it fought off attempts by high-street chain Costa Coffee to open a branch in the town. This victory sums up the community's strongly independent character, which is evident in its many cafés, restaurants and health-food shops. Here, sustainable ingredients – including local, organic vegetables and higher-welfare meat – as well as vegan and gluten-free foods are commonplace. So if you have specific dietary needs or simply care about the source of your food, you're likely to find what you're looking for in Totnes.

Topsham

These days, Topsham is classed as a suburb of Exeter, but it has a heart and soul that's very much its own. From its farm shops to its high-quality pubs and restaurants, there can be no doubt that food is taken very seriously here. But that's not all. Topsham also has a boozy side – the small community is home to the multi-award-winning Pebblebed Vineyards, which hosts tours and tastings.

Dorset is a dream destination for anyone in search of good food. With countless artisan producers setting up shop across the county in the past few years, you'll be spoilt for choice in just about every food category.

Although Dorset doesn't have the expansive coastline that Cornwall has, you'll find some of the southwest's best seafood restaurants here. Of special note is Rachel's in Bridport (see p.198), where you'll be served an incredible fish feast at a very reasonable price.

But the county's best-known edible export has to be the humble Dorset knob. Traditionally served with a hunk of cheese (although a generous knob of butter is just as delicious), these dry, crunchy biscuits are rather moreish. If you haven't tried them before, make a point of hunting them down.

Lyme Regis

It's hard not to fall in love with Lyme Regis, affectionately dubbed the Pearl of Dorset by locals. Made famous as the setting of John Fowles's 1969 novel, *The French Lieutenant's Woman*, this small town is an atmospheric, elemental place, where waves crash over the historic harbour wall (known as the Cobb) in stormy weather. Lyme is also known, these days, for its thriving food scene. Popular Aroma café (see p.76) caters to every taste and intolerance.

Shaftesbury

With picture-postcard views over Blackmore Vale and a wealth of restaurants and cafés known for their good food and service, the hilltop town of Shaftesbury is a highlight of the region. It was here, on steep, cobbled Gold Hill, that director Ridley Scott set his famous Hovis advert of the 1970s (see p.79).

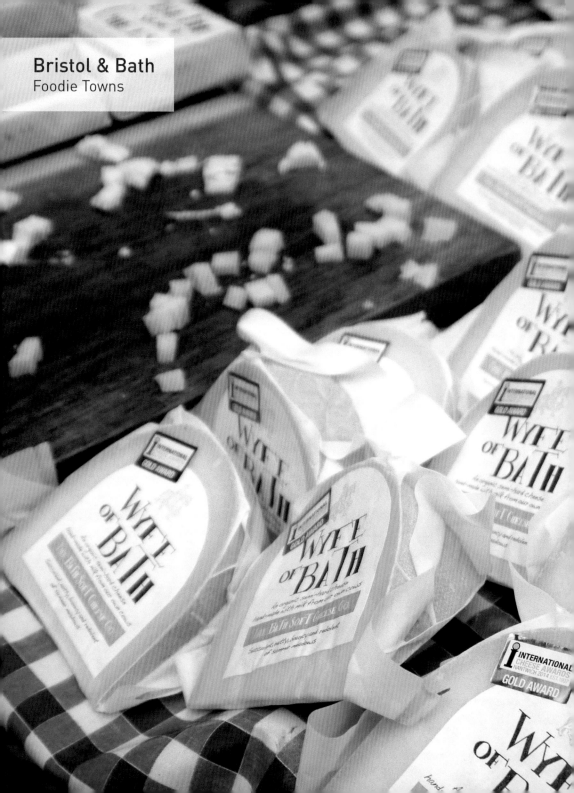

You'll never be far from a good meal in Bristol or Bath, which are magnets for the top growers and producers in the region.

Bristol has a well-deserved reputation for its sustainable-food scene, boasting all manner of earthy eateries. But the region's most famous and enduring culinary tradition has to be Bath chaps, which have been around since the days when the city was a major pork-trading centre. Made of pig's cheek and jawbone that has been brined, boiled and then chilled in a mould, this rich piece of meat may be served hot or cold. You'll see Bath chaps in restaurants all over the region, thanks to the recent revival in nose-to-tail eating.

St Nicholas Market, Bristol

You can munch your way around the world in this covered market (see pp.206–7), where sensational street-food vendors and artisan producers tout their global grub.

Clifton Village, Bristol

This affluent area of Bristol, perched on a hill overlooking the city, is fit to bursting with great places to eat and drink. Expect smart gastro pubs and high-end delis.

Bath Farmers' Market, Bath

This farmers' market (p.212) – the first to open in the UK – is the kind of place where you can relax with a newspaper and a strong coffee for hours against a backdrop of friendly banter.

Walcott Street, Bath

Pubs, cafés and local producers unite in this tasty corner of Bath, known locally as the Artisan Quarter. Take your time exploring its impressive range of independent retailers.

Somerset
Foodie Towns

Driving through the heart of England's orchard, you shouldn't be surprised if you see more apple trees than you can shake a stick at. It would be wrong not to indulge in some fruity goodness while you're here, from traditional scrumpy cider to more family-friendly juices. And if you visit in the autumn – the apple-pressing season – you'll notice the sweet scent of apples filling the air.

Another famous export from this beautiful county is Cheddar cheese. One of the nation's best-loved cheeses, Cheddar dates back to the late 12th century, when it was matured in the caves of Cheddar Gorge. Is it any wonder that Cheddar cheese and apples make such tasty companions in a traditional ploughman's lunch?

Glastonbury

Unsurprisingly, given its associations with the world-famous music festival that takes its name, the small town of Glastonbury offers a vibrant global food scene. Choose from any number of cafés here, most of which boast environmentally sound credentials and are vegetarian or vegan – though there's also plenty to keep die-hard meat-eaters happy.

Wells

The cathedral city of Wells packs a very big punch, from its historic architecture to its exceptional eateries. If you visit during the annual food festival, you'll be able to taste all kinds of edible delights from the 100 artisan producers who ply their wares from street stalls.

Frome

If you enjoy the buzz of a great food market, plan your visit to Frome to coincide with either the Farmers' Market or the Country Market. These are moveable feasts, so be sure to call into the tourist-information office (at The Library, on Justice Lane) for up-to-date information.

INDEX

page

Bakeries
At the Chapel 144
Da Bara Bakery.. 152
Mulberry Manor 161
Sarah's Pasty Shop 155
St Kew Harvest Farm Shop........................ 184
The Bakehouse 72
The Bakery 166
The Bertinet Bakery.................................... 170

Cafés
Aroma... 76
Bean Shot Coffee 143
Beggars' Banquet Café 82
Café at the Grain 146
Café de Ville 54
Café Ronak 110
Chapel Arts Centre Café 122
Cheese & Alfies... 94
Coast 88
Coast Coffee Bar and Bistro 16
Downhouse Farm Garden Café................. 196
Felicity's Farm Shop 195
Fern Pit Café 20
Full Court Press 107
Harbour House Café 60
Hartley's Kitchen.. 142
Heather's Coffee Shop 13
Home Farm Café... 65
John Peel Restaurant 83
Little Pickle 90
Lye Cross Farm Shop 216
Mother Meldrum's Tea Gardens 59

page

Mud Dock 108
Mulberry Manor 161
Pomegranate Café Restaurant 118
Pumpkin Delicatessen and Café.............. 172
ReLoved 78
Rock Pool Café... 48
Rock Salt Café and Brasserie..................... 46
Route 2 71
Scarlett's Garden Café 128
Silvers Pantry.. 130
Soukitchen 104
Square Edge Café 140
St Kew Harvest Farm Shop........................ 184
St Werburghs City Farm Café 112
Talland Bay Beach Café 36
The Apple Tree Café 12
The Bakehouse 72
The Bakery 166
The Birdcage 58
The Crafty Teacup Café 131
The Good Earth 176
The Hidden Hut 32
The Mall Deli 167
The Old Bookshop...................................... 106
The Salt Cellar 79
The Salt Pig 164
The Secret Garden Café 23
The Shed 127
The Thali Café 102
The Toucan Café... 126
The Trading Post 134
The Yellow Bicycle....................................... 84
Venue 35... 98

page

Venue 72...62
Westward Café and Truckstop....................55
Wildebeest 22
Woods Café 34
Yume Kitchen 105

Cookery Schools

Bordeaux Quay..228
Charles Dowding......................................230
Cheese & Alfies..94
Etherington's Butchery Academy 223
Fat Hen...222
Graze & Flavour.......................................224
Panary..226
Streamcombe Cookery School 229
The Bertinet Kitchen................................170
The Empire Farm 231
The Holt..225
The Tickled Pig...86
Vale House Kitchen 227

Delis and Markets

Bath Farmers' Market 210
Blacks Delicatessen 157
Brown and Forrest 171
Café de Ville 54
Darts Farm...192
Olives Et Al..162
Pumpkin Delicatessen and Café...............172
Queen Street Delicatessen 174
Silvers Pantry 130
The Better Food Company 208
The Fish Deli 158

page

The Mall Deli...167
The Salt Pig..164

Diners

Genève..87
Ruby Modern Diner...................................68
Strong Adolfos 28
The Tube Diner 114

Farms and Farm Shops

Darts Farm..192
Downhouse Farm Garden Café..................196
Eweleaze Farm 200
Felicity's Farm Shop 195
Kimbers' Farm Shop 215
Lye Cross Farm Shop 216
Pitney Farm Shop.....................................214
Riverford...189
Somerset Cider Brandy Company 212
St Kew Harvest Farm Shop 184
St Werburghs City Farm Café 112
The Better Food Company 208
The Salt Pig..164
The Trading Post 134
The Udder Farm Shop...............................202
Trevaskis Farm Shop 182

Foodie Towns

Bath...243
Bristol..243
Falmouth..237
Frome...245
Glastonbury..245

INDEX

page

Lyme Regis................................241
Newlyn 237
Padstow..................................237
Shaftesbury.............................241
Topsham.................................239
Totnes....................................239
Wells......................................245

Pubs and Bars
Beggars' Banquet Café.................82
Burgers and Barrels....................119
Early Doors 136
Fingle Bridge Inn 63
Masons Arms 35
Mud Dock 108
Pigs Nose Inn 64
The Bakehouse 72
The Clifton Sausage....................99
The Dolphin 85
The Kings Arms 33
The NoBody Inn.........................70
The Old Bookshop......................106
The Pig on the Hill 44
The Springer Spaniel 40
The White Post 77
Venue 35..................................98

Restaurants
At the Chapel 144
Brown and Forrest 171
Burgers and Barrels....................119
Darts Farm 192
Fatbelly Fred's...........................50

page

Goodfellows..............................137
Historical Dining Rooms...............111
Ocean & Earth...........................38
Pomegranate Café Restaurant.......118
Poolside Indulgence 15
RHS Rosemoor 49
Riverford..................................189
Rock Salt Café and Brasserie.........46
Terra Madre 52
The Bakehouse 72
The Bath Priory..........................120
The Clifton Sausage....................99
The Good Earth 176
The Idle Rocks...........................24
The Old Coastguard 14
The Oyster Shack........................56
The Pavilion Boatshed 18
The Thali Café 102
The Tickled Pig...........................86
The Udder Farm Shop..................202
Trevaskis Farm Shop 182
Venue 72..................................62
Wallfish Bistro............................100
Yume Kitchen 105

Street Food and Snacks
Barford Ice Cream Garden.............204
Eat a Pitta................................207
Funghi Fruits.............................211
Inkie's Smokehouse BBQ...............188
Kernow Forno 186
Mulberry Manor 161
Oasis Falafel and Grill 194

page

PJ's Ice Cream Parlour 132
Rachel's 198
Sarah's Pasty Shop 155
Seadog 190
Soukitchen 104
The Bristol Sausage Shop 206
The Cornish Maids Fudge Shop.................154
The Steak Out...205

Suppliers

Brown and Forrest 171
Country Cheeses...156
Dartmoor Butchers.....................................160
Funghi Fruits..211
Riverford...189
Somerset Cider Brandy Company 212

page

The Bristol Sausage Shop 206
The Cornish Maids Fudge Shop.................154
The Fine Cheese Co. 168

Tearooms and Gardens

Barford Ice Cream Garden.........................204
Comins Tea House 80
Downhouse Farm Garden Café..................196
Heather's Coffee Shop 13
Heligan Tearoom...30
Mother Meldrum's Tea Gardens 59
Rectory Farm Tea Rooms 187
ReLoved 78
The Bath Priory..120
The Birdcage 58
The Blitz Tearoom 133

BEST VENUES FOR...

...VALUE

	page
Rock Salt Café and Brasserie	46
The Yellow Bicycle	84
Westward Café and Truckstop	55
The Good Earth	176
John Peel Restaurant	83
At the Chapel	144

...GORGEOUS VIEWS

	page
The Salt Cellar	79
Felicity's Farm Shop	195
Fingle Bridge Inn	63
Fern Pit Café	20
Early Doors	136
The White Post	77

...MEAT

	page
Inkie's Smokehouse BBQ	188
The Bristol Sausage Shop	206
Burgers and Barrels	119
Ruby Modern Diner	68
Trevaskis Farm Shop	182
The Salt Pig	164

...VEGAN FOOD

	page
Wildebeest	22
Eat a Pitta	207
Harbour House Café	60
Beggars' Banquet Café	82
The Better Food Company	208
Café Ronak	110

...FISH & SEAFOOD

	page
Rachel's	198
The Oyster Shack	56
The Fish Deli	158
The Pavilion Boatshed	18
Brown and Forrest	171
Yume Kitchen	105

...ROMANCE

	page
The Tickled Pig	86
The NoBody Inn	70
The Bath Priory	120
Wallfish Bistro	100
The Bakehouse	72
The Birdcage	58

BEST VENUES FOR...

...FAMILY FUN

	page
Barford Ice Cream Garden	204
Trevaskis Farm Shop	182
The Crafty Teacup Café	131
Café at the Grain	146
PJ's Ice Cream Parlour	132
Venue 35	98

...TRADITIONAL CUISINE

	page
Soukitchen (Middle Eastern)	104
Historical Dining Rooms (old English)	111
Ocean & Earth (Thai)	38
The Thali Café (Indian)	102
Comins Tea House (Japanese)	80
The Blitz Tearoom (wartime British)	133

...PEOPLE WATCHING

	page
Eweleaze Farm	200
Aroma	76
The Old Bookshop	106
Coast	88
Cheese & Alfies	94
The Shed	127

...SUSTAINABILITY

	page
Riverford	189
Heligan Tearoom	30
Funghi Fruits	211
The Trading Post	134
St Werburghs City Farm Café	112
Bath Farmers' Market	210

...WALKING

	page
Rectory Farm Tea Rooms	187
Woods Café	34
Talland Bay Beach Café	36
Pigs Nose Inn	64
Mother Meldrum's Tea Gardens	59
Downhouse Farm Garden Café	196

...COFFEE

	page
Full Court Press	107
Bean Shot Coffee	143
Mud Dock	108
Coast Coffee Bar and Bistro	16
Route 2	71
Scarlett's Garden Café	128

ACKNOWLEDGEMENTS

The Secret Seeker team love eating and drinking just as much as they love hunting for secret coves and hidden beaches, so a food and restaurant guide was the obvious next step after the success of *Secret Beaches: Southwest England*. And what a lot of fun it has been, from savouring cream teas to sampling the finest home-cured gravadlax, with more than a few Cornish pasties scoffed along the way.

Many thanks to all the venues who were so kind to Jane and welcomed her in to take photos and sample their delicious food. Thanks also to everyone in the production team, especially Jo Kirby, Becky Fountain, Alex Whittleton, Ben Hoo, Simon Borrough and Nicola Erdpresser for making this, the first book in the Secret Kitchen series, possible. But above all thanks to Jane Sarchet for her excellent research and tireless enthusiasm for eating and drinking her way around the West Country.

JANE SARCHET

Back in 2008, Jane started a blog about her life on a small Cornish farm called Hedgecombers.com. In the years since, the blog has turned into a large website with several hundred unique recipes and articles on everything from rearing Muscovy ducks to how to make coconut milk.

As the website evolved, the photography aspect of it became more and more important, so in her late 30's, Jane took herself back to school to study photography, with the ultimate aim of making people hungry by looking at her pictures.

When Jane's not out scouring the UK to find great and unusual places to eat for Secret Seeker, or shooting tasty images for restaurants and artisan producers, she can usually be found in the kitchen dreaming up new ways to put flavours together. You can find Jane all over social media as Hedgecomber and she'd love it if you came and said hi.

JANE'S ACKNOWLEDGEMENTS

Huge thanks go out to everyone that played a part, whether large or small, in getting the information for this book together.

Special thanks to all people who shared their favourite foodie haunts with such passion and the countless strangers that helped me with directions when on the road. To Susie, a good family friend who put me up for several nights in her beautiful home in Dorset over a Bank Holiday weekend when all the campsites were at bursting point. And to my lovely Mum Elaine, and my partner Jonny, for taking care of all the animals in my absence.

And finally to the team behind the real work of this book: Ben, the designer who showed endless patience, Katie for correcting my inevitable typos and the wonderful Becky who was the glue that held us all together and kept us (mostly) sane!

And finally to Rob Smith, the Publisher, who gave me the opportunity of a lifetime and sent me on a real foodie adventure.